TWENTIETH CENTURY BRITAIN

Jon Nichol

with Jane Skinner and Tony Andrews

Basil Blackwell

CONTENTS

For Eleanor, who will be 21 in the year 2000.

Foreword

This book, along with *The Twentieth Century World* in this series, intends to give readers an historical perspective on the society in which they live. An historical frame of reference affects all our lives – how we think and act, our beliefs and values. If in our schools we do not help provide pupils with an historical frame of reference, the outside world will. At its worst this can lead to riots in our cities, and the religious and racial violence that has torn Northern Ireland apart since 1969.

Our history is a *moral* issue – it is our shield and protector, the defender of our laws, our liberties and our rights. It shows where we have come from, what we should cherish, protect and discard. It is a lantern hanging over the bows of our ship – it cannot predict, but it can help guide us through the future.

This book is centred on the individual pupil. It starts from where the individual is today, and how he or she has got there in terms of family, home and neighbours. Then the book works outward to a more general look at our society. The last two sections look at a theme – Britain at War – and a topic – the Irish Question.

Twentieth Century Britain does *not* deal with Britain and the modern world – the wider perspective against which we can make sense of the nation's story. This vital aspect of our recent past is dealt with in *The Twentieth Century World* – the companion volume in this series.

Jon Nichol
School of Education, University of Exeter

INTRODUCTION

Most of us are British. We may even think of ourselves as being English, Irish, Scottish or Welsh. I am a Briton because of what I know and feel about my country's past. Such knowledge comes from the thousands of facts I have learned from reading books, newspapers and magazines, from watching TV and listening to radio and from what people tell me.

Our world has seen many changes since 1900. All around you is *evidence* of these changes — in the home, at school and in the towns and countryside. In his book *Down Memory Lane* Kenneth Bareham, born in 1905, writes:

A *It would be interesting to ask the younger reader if she would like — or, indeed, could even imagine, growing up in a world with no television, no radio, no recorders or record-players, no aeroplanes (for those holidays on the continent) no coaches or buses, no cars (there were perhaps only a dozen in the whole of the Tiverton area and they were slow, noisy and — yes — very smelly things), no bicycles, no watches and no cameras except for those heavy wooden, box-like things seen at the photographers. Electricity not having — as the saying goes — been 'heard of' there was, of course, no cinema.*

This book aims to help you understand the country in which you live. Each person, place or thing has its *history*. When we look out of the window or watch television the history we know helps us make sense of what we see and hear. Pages 4-23 ask how things in all our lives have changed over the past 80 years — our families, the home, school and education, our neighbourhoods and the world of work. Pages 24-59 look at the changes in many aspects of our society since 1900. These topics range from *The Royal Family* to *Britain at War*. Pages 60-63 enquire into a conflict which affects all our lives — *Ireland*. This book *does not* deal with Britain's role in Europe and the wider world. These topics are written about in another book to be read alongside this one — *The Twentieth Century World*.

One aim of *Twentieth Century Britain* is to encourage you to become your own historian. This means finding lots of clues from the past and thinking about them. We use such clues to work out what we know about our history. **B** is one such clue. What is the photograph about? When was it taken? What does it tell us about the people in it? How useful a source is it for an historian? What other questions would you like to ask about the picture? How could you find out more about the scene in **B**?

History is about asking questions to find out about the past. The questions above about **B** are the first of many we will ask. Often there are no right answers — but what we say should be based upon the *evidence* that we have.

B

ROOTS

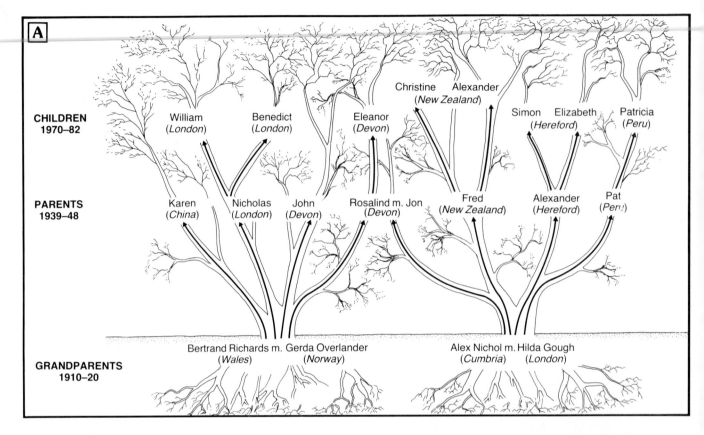

CHILDREN 1970–82
William (*London*) Benedict (*London*) Eleanor (*Devon*) Christine Alexander (*New Zealand*) Simon Elizabeth (*Hereford*) Patricia (*Peru*)

PARENTS 1939–48
Karen (*China*) Nicholas (*London*) John (*Devon*) Rosalind m. Jon (*Devon*) Fred (*New Zealand*) Alexander (*Hereford*) Pat (*Peru*)

GRANDPARENTS 1910–20
Bertrand Richards m. Gerda Overlander (*Wales*) (*Norway*)   Alex Nichol m. Hilda Gough (*Cumbria*) (*London*)

All of us have *roots* in the past. Our roots are our own histories and those of our families, friends, neighbours and the people we live and work with.

Most of us have widespread roots. **A** shows my family tree, with its roots and branches. As you can see, my family's roots are in Cumbria, London, Wales and Norway. It now has branches in China, Peru and New Zealand, as well as in England.

Your own roots, and those of your friends, could cover Britain and many other countries in the world. Britain is made up of millions of families whose roots and branches are linked together.

At home, you may have photographs like **B** and **C** showing events from your own past and that of your family and friends. All of us can remember things about our past. The memories of old people can go back a long way. George Brown, a famous politician, tells us:

D *On 2 September 1914, just one month after the outbreak of war, I was born in 1 Block,*

Peabody Buildings, Duke Street, Lambeth, from which we moved when I was six months old to Peabody Square, Blackfriars Road, Southwark. We had just two rooms, with no wash basins or bath. There was a communal sink on a landing, and one of my earliest memories is of seeing the light shining over Big Ben from the landing when I went out to wash.

My father's side of the family is from Ireland. My grandfather came over from Cork I believe at a very early age, and settled in south-east London. He was a butcher by trade, though he never had his own shop. My memory of him is slight, but I recall him as an enormous man and fond of his pleasures. I was very much afraid of him, although he was always kindly to children.

My father was born in London. He joined the Army Service Corps in 1915 and became an army driver, acting as chauffeur to a number of generals and other high ranking officers. He also learned to drive heavy lorries. When he came out of the army he got a job with Lyons, driving one of their lorries to deliver cakes and bread to their shops. I have the happiest memories of driving round with him on Sundays and getting cakes and chocolate buns at every shop where the manageress took a fancy to me.

Another early memory is of the weekly visit I used to pay to Wood's Eel and Pie Shop in The Cut to buy the pies which were eaten with something I have only ever had in an eel-pie shop, a rather wonderful parsley gravy which to this day I enjoy as much as the pies. The cost of these delicious pies was (if I remember rightly) twopence.

? ? ? ? ? ? ? ? ? ? ? ?

1 Copy maps of Britain and the world. Now mark on them the places where members of your family live or have lived in the past.

2 a Bring in the earliest photograph you can find of yourself. The form can hold a baby judging competition — the winner is the person who matches most photographs with members of the form.
b What do the photographs tell you about how babies were reared ten years or more ago? Compare them with **B**, a picture of a baby in 1900.

3 Write a story like **D** about your own early memories. Note down the things which you think might interest *your* grandchildren in 50 years time.

4 a List the evidence which clues **A-D** contain about how life has changed in the past 80 years in Britain.
b How far can we trust **C** and **D** as sources of history?

FAMILY LIFE 1900-50

A   *There's certainly been a change. I whack mine now, but not the beatings like we used to have. When I was a boy most of us feared our fathers more than we liked them. I know I feared mine and I had plenty of reason to.*

The man in **A** was remembering his childhood in Bethnal Green, London. **B** and **C** are two more memories of growing up there:

B   *I had a very strict father although he drank. When I came home from school at dinner time he put me to work making the dolls. When I got back again at tea-time he started me on it all again until seven when I went to bed. On Saturday nights we had to crawl under the table to get out of his way.*

C   *Men like my father never did much around the house. He found it a strain to pour out a cup of tea. If he saw a man pushing a pram or carrying a kiddy, he'd say he was a cissy. It's all changed now.*

D and **E** show more clues about family life before 1951. Elizabeth Armstrong was the daughter of a mine-worker. She was born in 1898. In **F** Elizabeth talks about life at home:

F   *We had a rather nice house but very small. Only two bedrooms and it was three storeys, so you went through one bedroom up the attic stairs to the top one. When I was a girl at home there wasn't a lot to do, just being two rooms up and a kitchen and a back kitchen and back yard. I had to dust and such as that and wash dishes, things that lasses have never liked, and do a bit of knitting and that. We played in the street. We would all get together of a night*

E

but, mind, we weren't allowed to play out late. We were in by seven o'clock and in bed, regular.

My father was always jobbing about the house and he was able – you know, if the fireplace wasn't right, he was able to do them sort of jobs and he kept everything tidy. But he never did any washing up. That was below him, such as that. But he cleaned the shoes every Sunday morning – no, every Monday morning after the Sunday.

We only had meat once a week. We only got it on Sundays when we had a hot dinner with Father and Mother. The rest of the week, what meat was left was for my Father because he needed good feed because of his hard job. We had bread and butter and jam and porridge and such as that and we got taties every day. Maybe bacon and something of that sort. Very often not any bacon or meat either, just taties and pudding – mostly rice pudding. . .milk was only a penny halfpenny a pint in them days.

Mother made a lot of pea soups and such as that. So we got good stuff but it was very plain. And we got kippers and maybe an egg. Sometimes we got the top off the egg and that was all. We never wanted for a slice of bread.

?????????????????????????????????

1 Look at **D** and **E**. Now mark where you think each family comes on the five point scale below. For example, if you think the people in **D** look well fed, put **D** under 5 in that column, and so on.

```
              1 2 3 4 5
badly educated — — — — — well educated
 badly clothed — — — — — well clothed
          poor — — — — — rich
     unhealthy — — — — — healthy
        hungry — — — — — well fed
         dirty — — — — — clean
           sad — — — — — happy
```

2 List ten things you can see in **D**. What similar things would you expect to see in a house today? Explain the changes.

3 For each piece of evidence **A**-**F**, say whether you think it is about a working class, middle class or upper class family. Give reasons for your answers.

4 Interview someone over 50 years old about family life when they were young. Ask them about their homes, their food and clothing, the games they played, discipline, their friends. . .

FAMILY LIFE 1950-80

A

Come, mothers and fathers, throughout the land.
And don't criticise what you can't understand.
Your sons and daughters are beyond your command.
Your old world is rapidly ageing.
Please get out of the new one if you can't lend your hand,
For the times, they are a-changing.

(A pop song of the 1960s by Bob Dylan)

Since 1950 a major change in family life has been the huge increase in freedom for young people, **A**. With their own money to spend on things like pop music, clothes, holidays, record and cassette players, the young are much better off than before 1950. Scenes like **B** only became common in the late 1950s. Some young people dressed in new ways — Teddy Boys like **C** in the 1950s, Mods and Rockers in the 1960s and Punks in the 1970s. But in 1974 a survey of 10 000 16-year-olds showed that they had *the same* beliefs about family life as their parents and grandparents.

A second major change in family life has been the huge increase in divorce, **D**. Before 1950 there were few, as it was very hard to get a divorce. Since the 1969 Divorce Reform Act there has been a massive rise in the number of divorces. Each year some 3 out of a 100 marriages break up. Now a couple can get divorced if they can show the marriage has broken down and cannot be mended.

A third change in family life has been the sharp drop in the size of families. In 1900 the birth rate per thousand of the population was 28; in 1920, 20; in 1940, 16; in 1960, 16 and in 1980, 13. After 1962 the contraceptive pill became common. It freed women from the problems which Mrs. Florence of Bethnal Green, London talked about in 1957:

B

C

children if you didn't want to have them. And if the woman complained, it was hold your noise and give her another baby, and that's the finish.

Many families' lives have been changed by moving to new housing estates and new towns. Sometimes, this has meant the breakdown of the close family ties that existed in places like the East End of London, where Mr Robbins lived:

F *I've got my drinking friends, that's my brothers-in-law mostly. We're a proper mixing family. I see the wife's mother at least once every day and most of her sisters and my brothers-in-law too. All the brothers-in-law go out together — mix in the same company, use the same pubs, have the same activities, follow the same sports. At the week-ends we all take our wives along when we can, so it's a real family gathering.*

E *Fifty years ago it was different. They had more children than they could afford. The pubs were open all day, so far as I can understand. The man would spend all his money in the pub, come home and abuse his wife. There was no birth control in those days, I know, but even then there were ways and means not to have*

D **Divorces in Britain, 1905 – 1984**

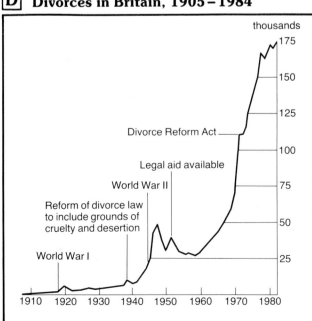

thousands

- Divorce Reform Act
- Legal aid available
- World War II
- Reform of divorce law to include grounds of cruelty and desertion
- World War I

175
150
125
100
75
50
25

1910 1920 1930 1940 1950 1960 1970 1980

???????????

1 a How might young people like those in **B** have spent their free time in the 1920s?
b What ideas about them do you think the young men in **C** wanted the photographer to have? What do their clothes, hair-cuts and the way they stand tell us about them?
c What does **D** suggest about the growth of divorce?
d What does the evidence tell us about changes in family size since 1911?

2 Interview someone between the ages of 20 and 50 about how they were treated as teenagers. Ask them what they can remember about *changes* in the way in which young people are treated and brought up in the past 40 years: punishments, pocket money, entertainment and games, school, home life and so on.

3 If the following had moved to a modern housing estate from London, what might they tell you about changes in their life since the 1960s: the people in **B** and **C**; Mrs Florence in **E**; Mr Robbins in **F**?

4 Write notes or paragraphs on how family life has changed since 1900. Mention: children, their play; teenagers; birth control and family size; divorce; family togetherness; family ideals.

THE HOME

A is an advertisement for the latest labour-saving device of the 1920s. **B** shows what the 'ideal' family sitting room might have looked like in the 1950s. **C** is a fully-equipped modern kitchen. These pictures are all clues about how our homes have changed since 1900.

The machines and inventions in **D** have made life easier and more enjoyable for millions of people. Almost every home in Britain now has electricity. Electric-powered equipment like vacuum cleaners, washing machines, refrigerators and food mixers takes much of the hard work out of running a home.

In 1949 my family moved to a new house in the country:

E *We had to carry water in buckets from the village pump. There was no electricity. So we used a solid fuel stove and cooked on paraffin*

C

rings. *Light came from paraffin lamps — Tilley lamps — and candles. Our new radio worked off batteries, and we had no television. Stairs and carpets had to be brushed with a dustpan and brush, for there was no hoover. Washing day, Monday, was hard, sweaty work. Huge pans of boiling water were poured into the dolly tub, and mother had to swirl the clothes around with the dolly stick to get the dirt off. There was only bar soap — no modern washing powder. A big problem in summer was to keep food from going bad, because we had no fridge. We used to put butter and milk in a bucket half full of cold water, with a cloth draped over the milk can and the butter dish.*

In the next 20 years we got electricity, an electric cooker, fridge, hoover, toaster, washing machine, tape recorder, record player and many other things which made life much easier.

D **Time line of main changes in the home**

1900	Paraffin and gas lighting common.
1920	Gas and electricity in new houses and spreading to older houses.
1922	BBC set up with monopoly for radio broadcasting.
1930s	Spread of wireless to most homes.
1940s	Electrical appliances common in most homes — particularly vacuum cleaners and electric irons. Spread of TV. Only 2% of homes had fridges.
1955	Independent Television founded.
1956	4 out of 5 homes had TV.
1960s	Telephones, fridges, washing machines become common.
1967	Introduction of colour TV.
1970s	Colour TV common. Spread of cassette recorders.
1980s	Video recorders, computers in the home.

? ? ? ? ? ? ? ? ? ? ?

1 Make out a table to show how the sitting room in **B** would have to change to become an 'ideal' room today. What new objects would you put in it?

2 Think of what you do during an ordinary day. How many things from list **D** do you use? Now make out a diary of what might happen if you could not use any of these things.

3 Using **D**, make out a questionnaire to find out when people first had these objects in their homes.

4 **A** and **C** come from advertisements. How useful are advertisements to the historian? Can we trust what they say? What problems can you think of, in using them as historical *evidence*?

HOUSING 1900-80

A

Do you go past any houses like **A** on your way to school? In the nineteenth century most big towns had many streets like this. Often the houses were badly built and overcrowded, and they quickly became slums. Since 1900 local and central governments have tried to improve housing. Many of the slum areas have been knocked down − slum clearance − and the people re-housed in new council houses or blocks of flats. But even today many people do not have decent places to live. Charities like *Shelter* have been set up to try and find places for the homeless.

In 1900 most people lived in their own houses or rented homes from private landlords. The first major move by government to build new houses came after the First World War (1914-18). The Prime Minister, Lloyd George, had promised to provide 'Homes fit for heroes' for the returning troops. In 1919 Parliament passed an Act to get local government to build working class homes. The Act led to the first *council estates*, **B**. Since 1919 local councils in most towns have built council estates. Private firms have also built houses for sale.

After the Second World War (1939-45) there was another huge demand for housing from returning troops who wanted to start families. There were long waiting lists for houses, and although the government built over 200 000 houses a year there were still not enough. Not until the 1950s could private builders and local authorities supply homes for almost everyone.

Many towns grew quickly in the 1940s and 50s. Also New Towns were planned and built in the countryside or on wasteland, **C**. The New Towns had all the things which people wanted. There were separate places for work, leisure, living, shopping and transport. Planners also tried hard to keep people and motor cars apart. Not everyone liked the new towns and estates. Some people felt cut off and lonely, like Mrs Sandeman, who said:

D *When I first came I cried for weeks, it was so lonely. It was a shock to see such a steep hill going up to the shops.*

E is a description of the new estate Mrs Sandeman lived on:

E *Less than twenty miles away from*

B

Bethnal Green (London) the automatic doors of the tube train open on to the new land of Greenleigh. On one side of the railway are cows at pasture. On the other, the new housing estate. Instead of the shops of Bethnal Green there is the shopping centre at the Parade: instead of the street barrows piled high with fruit, fish, and dresses. . . there are the orderly self-service stores — the marble halls of the great firms (Tesco, Sainsburys, etc.) In place of the gaunt buildings rising above narrow streets there are up-to-date semi-detached homes. Greenleigh belongs firmly to the taste of this mid-century. Built since the war to a single plan, it is all of one piece. Though the council has mixed different types of houses, row upon row

look almost identical, each beside a concrete road, each enclosed by a fence, each with its little patch of flower garden at front and larger patch of vegetable garden at back, each with expansive front windows covered with net curtains. All built, owned and guarded by a single landlord.　(from *Family and Kinship in East London*, Michael Young and Peter Willmott, 1957)

? ? ? ? ? ? ? ? ? ? ?

1　a What *five* reasons might there be for pulling down the houses in **A** — put these in your order of importance.
　b Why might the housing in **B** be better than that in **A**? How might it be *worse*?

2 If you interviewed a working class housewife in one of the houses in **A** before and after she moved to a new house in **B**, what might she tell you about:
　a The state of her home — furniture, walls, baths, taps, damp, noise.
　b Ties with friends, neighbours, family
　c How she spends her time
　d Pubs, shops, markets, cinemas etc.

3 Carry out a survey of housing between your home and school, looking for:
　Council estates built from 1920-40; 1945-70
　Private estates built from 1900-40; 1945-80
　How have these houses changed?
Interview someone who has lived for over 20 years in a house near yours, and ask them about how they felt about their house and neighbours when they moved, and how the area has changed since.

C　**New Towns in Britain**

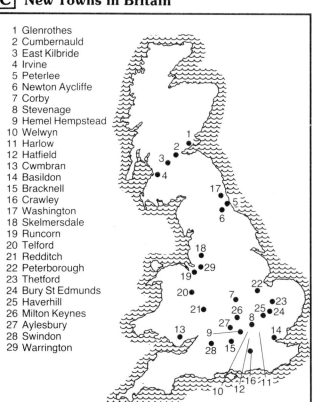

1 Glenrothes
2 Cumbernauld
3 East Kilbride
4 Irvine
5 Peterlee
6 Newton Aycliffe
7 Corby
8 Stevenage
9 Hemel Hempstead
10 Welwyn
11 Harlow
12 Hatfield
13 Cwmbran
14 Basildon
15 Bracknell
16 Crawley
17 Washington
18 Skelmersdale
19 Runcorn
20 Telford
21 Redditch
22 Peterborough
23 Thetford
24 Bury St Edmunds
25 Haverhill
26 Milton Keynes
27 Aylesbury
28 Swindon
29 Warrington

DRESS AND FASHION

Pictures **A** to **D** give some ideas about how dress and fashion have changed since 1900. Before the 1950s only rich people could afford to buy smart, new clothes. Today, all of us can buy cheap copies of the latest fashions, thanks to chain stores like Marks and Spencer or Littlewoods, and mail order catalogues.

During the 1960s there was a revolution in the dress of young people. New materials like denim, man-made fibres and plastics were used along with old-fashioned wool and cotton cloth. Styles changed quickly. During the 1960s most young people began to wear new kinds of clothes — jeans, cords, denim, plastics and mini skirts. Carnaby Street and the King's Road, Chelsea, were where the young flocked to buy the new kinds of clothes. I still remember the thrill in 1965 of going down the King's Road, looking at the clothes in the shops and the smart fashions of the crowd milling along the pavement. By the mid-1960s every town had its 'boutiques' and clothes shops selling the new, casual fashion — fashion that was brought into every house by TV programmes like *Ready Steady Go*, *The Avengers* and *Top of the Pops*.

A

B

Today, styles change so quickly that there is no single 'fashionable' way to dress. You can all buy smart clothes in supermarkets and High Street shops. Most people choose clothes to suit their tastes or lifestyle. Some even look back to the past, and wear the kinds of clothes that were fashionable in the 1920s or '50s.

1 Would you like to dress like the people in **C** or **D**? Choose either the man in **D** or the woman in **C** and make a table comparing their clothes with yours. Describe each item, and say what it is made of and how comfortable it looks.

2 Look at the women in **A**. How do their clothes differ from the ones in **C**? What does this suggest about the women's lives?

3 Put pictures **A – D** into date order, starting with the oldest. What clues can you see in each picture to help you? If you have a school uniform, which period does it come from?

4 Look at the young people in **B**. What do their clothes tell you about them? What do you think your clothes tell other people about you?

5 Hold a parade of fashions from the past 80 years from clothes you have at home, or mount a picture display showing changes in dress from home books, photographs, magazines or what you can find in the library.

ENTERTAINMENT

Read a newspaper. What does it tell you about how we pass our spare time and the things we enjoy doing? Today, most people have more leisure time and more money to spend on entertainment than ever before. And there are many more ways to spend that time and money than in 1900.

Since 1900 leisure and entertainment have changed because of new inventions like film, radio and television; the increase in the amount of money people have to spend; new forms of travel like the motor car and aeroplane; longer holidays and shorter working weeks.

If you had been at school in 1900 you would have had to make your own entertainment. At home some people held 'musical evenings' or passed the time playing games and reading aloud. Rich people might own one of the new gramophones and listen to recordings of songs, music and speeches. Sometimes there would be 'live' shows at a local theatre or music hall, and sporting events – like football or cricket matches. The train meant that families who could afford a holiday might travel to a seaside resort like Blackpool, **A**.

B describes how children spent their leisure time in the 1920s:

B *Once school was over we had our little select gang and we didn't bother anybody. Well, we had the little river, the Bob beck as we called it, to play in and one thing and another. And there again it was our own little area. We never got into any serious trouble. I mean, we used to rob orchards and things like this which was the*

A

way of life in those days. We used to go to the pictures once a week. We used to make our own enjoyment because there was more then. Everything was seasonal and you used to find that it cost you nothing to get a hoop or a whip and a top. The girls had hoppy bed and skipping and one thing and another and it was all on a no cost basis because it was the only way you could work it. Yet we wanted for nothing to do. Never in the house.

In the 1920s many people went to the cinema to see silent films with stars like Charlie Chaplin. The first 'talkies' (films with sound) were brought out in the 1930s. Soon every town had its own cinema, **C**. Many are still there, although they have often been turned into bingo halls. In the 1930s Hollywood was at its height as the centre of the film making industry.

During the 1920s radio broadcasting also began. The BBC (British Broadcasting Corporation) was set up to provide radio programmes for Britain. In the 1930s television broadcasts started – at first to tiny audiences.

The rise of television since the Second World War has totally changed the way most of us spend our leisure time. In 1955 a second TV network, ITV, was set up. Now there are four channels, offering an even wider choice – and cable television is on the way. Videos, stereos, cassette recorders and home computers also provide entertainment within the home. As a result, old forms of entertainment like going to the cinema or music hall, and attending football matches, have become less popular. Many cinemas and theatres have had to close down.

Today, many children spend more time watching television than they spend in school.

The traditional British holiday at the seaside has declined since the 1960s. Cheap air travel and 'package' holidays have meant that many people can afford to go abroad instead of holidaying at the British resorts.

? ? ? ? ? ? ? ? ? ? ?

1 When could you first:
   a go to the cinema?
   b listen to the BBC?
   c watch ITV?

2 a Look at **A**. What sort of things could you do at Blackpool in the 1900s?
   b Design a poster to get people to go to a British seaside resort today.

3 Write a diary about your day after you get home from school. How long do you spend doing homework, playing, watching television? How does the way you spend your leisure time compare with the children in **B**?

PEOPLE AND CLASS

'I always wanted to get out of the working class,' said my friend in his posh accent. After grammar school and university he had become a university lecturer. His father still worked in the ship-yards at Newcastle. All of us have feelings about which *class* we belong to. Some people are proud of their family background. Other people want to escape from the class they were born into as soon as they can.

At the start of the century it was clear which class you belonged to.

A *It was a world in which it was easy to distinguish the classes into which society was divided, for every class had its own dress. Our modest household included a resident cook, two maids and a nurse as well as a part time laundress.*

(from *The Lion and the Unicorn*, by Arthur Bryant, 1969)

The historian Arthur Bryant, who wrote **A**, came from a well-off home. People from working-class homes would often become servants to rich families. Richard Lowther looked after two rich boys in the 1930s:

B *They were eighteen. About my age . . . They had fantastic wardrobes. They would have morning clothes, perhaps three suits at that, and then they would have various lounge suits for the afternoon. It was a very busy life because they had a clean shirt on every time. Perhaps six shirts a day.*

You took them a cup of tea in the morning at eight o'clock. Huge bedrooms, they had, and dressing rooms. You would say to them, what would you be wearing today? What's your pro-gramme for today? And they would tell you.

Well, where they would be going — perhaps an afternoon party. . . . It was a life that buzzed with social events there. You got a lot of tickets given to you with the lady's maids to go. You see, you never mixed with the ordinary ser-vants. You lived in the housekeeper's room.

The butler, and under-butler and the valets and the housekeeper and the head cook, they fed by themselves.

Strong feelings remained about class into the 1950s. **C** is what some people said in 1959 on a private housing estate in Woodford, North London.

C Mr Burgess: *The working class live on the other side of Well Road but not this side.*

Mr Day: *The railway line is the dividing line — those who live below are not thought of as being as high class as those who live above.*

Retired couple: *On both sides they're from the East End. That's what has really made us decide to retire to Worthing. You can't talk to those people, we just don't speak the same language.*

Working class man: *The middle-class people here are snobs. They put on airs and graces. They are all out for show — nothing in their stomachs but nice suits on.*

Since the 1950s the clear divisions between the classes have become blurred. We can no longer tell which class a person comes from just by the clothes he or she wears or how they speak. Some people say that Britain has become a 'classless' society. What do you think?

? ? ? ? ? ? ? ? ? ? ? ?

1 Draw up a chart to show into which class (upper, upper middle, middle, lower middle, working) you would place: yourself; your oldest living relative; Mr Day; Arthur Bryant; Richard Lowther; the twin boys. Give reasons for your answers.

2 a Compare how you get up and the clothes you wear with the two boys in **B**. What do their lives tell you about the upper classes before the Second World War?
b What might the boy in **A** think of the twins?

3 Look at what the retired couple and the working class man say in **C**. Do you think they are being fair? How would *you* explain the terms 'working class', 'middle class' and 'upper class'?

WOMEN AND WORK

A

NO right to vote in general elections

NO chance to become a solicitor, accountant, senior civil servant, MP

NO right to equal pay for doing the same job as other people

NO way of improving working conditions, long hours, low pay

How would you feel if when you grew up all the points in **A** were true? If your great-grandmother was born before 1900 this is what the future could have held for her. Before 1918 women were *discriminated* against, simply for being women. They had almost no chance of getting well-paid or interesting jobs, **B**.

After 1900 many women were becoming angry about this. They demanded the right to be treated in the same way as men. One group was determined to win the right to vote. They were called Suffragettes (*suffrage* means the right to vote).

The biggest step forward for women came during the First World War, 1914-18. Women played a major part in the war effort, and took over many of the jobs of the men who were away fighting, see **C**. In 1919 women over 30 won the vote, largely because of their war work, when they showed they were men's equals.

B **Women's jobs in 1901**

The 1901 Devon census shows that out of 282 767 women in the county 67 027 had jobs.

	Unmarried	Married
Domestic servants	37 558	7 611
Dressmakers	12 698	3 293
Teachers	3 442	336
Nurses	811	851
Lawyers, engineers, accountants	0	0
Physicians, surgeons	3	0
Officers of commercial company/guild/society	4	0

From the 1920s the spread of inventions like the hoover and washing machine meant women's work in the home became easier. More and more women took full-time jobs – although these were often unskilled. In the 1960s and 1970s women began to do new kinds of work. Women also began to feel free to lead their own kinds of lives, and books on women's rights were read widely. A movement gained widespread support to give women equal pay for the same work as men and an equal right to do the same kinds of jobs. In 1975 Parliament passed the Sex Discrimination Act and set up an Equal Opportunities Commission. 1979 saw Margaret Thatcher's election as Britain's first woman Prime Minister.

C

??????????????

1 Use **B** to help you fill in the chart below. Put a tick under what you think is the best answer. In 1900, what were a woman's chances of becoming:

	very good	good	poor	nil
nurse				
doctor				
servant				
teacher				
solicitor				
Prime Minister				

Now put a cross under what you think today.

2 Interview a man and a woman between the ages of 50 and 60 about how women's lives have changed. Ask about education, work, marriage, leisure. . . Now compare the answers. What do they suggest about attitudes to women?

SUFFRAGETTES

Look at **A**. What is going on? The picture was taken at Epsom racecourse during the running of the Derby in June 1913. One of the people on the ground was Emily Davison. She had just flung herself under one of the horse's hooves, and brought it crashing to the ground. Later she was to die in hospital. Why did she bring down the horse?

Emily Davison was a *suffragette*. For years she and many other women had been fighting to win the vote for women. They fought in many ways. They set letter boxes on fire, smashed shop windows and even attacked leading politicians like Lloyd-George, the Chancellor of the Exchequer. **B** was written by his son, Richard:

B *The militant suffragettes showed their hysteria by planting a bomb in our home, which wrecked four rooms. One of the women threw a steel spike through the window of father's cab. It missed his eye by a fraction and pierced his cheek.*

Some of the suffragettes were arrested, see **C**. They were sent to prison, where many went on hunger strike and were force fed, **D**. The government did not dare let them starve to death, so it set free those in danger of dying. But

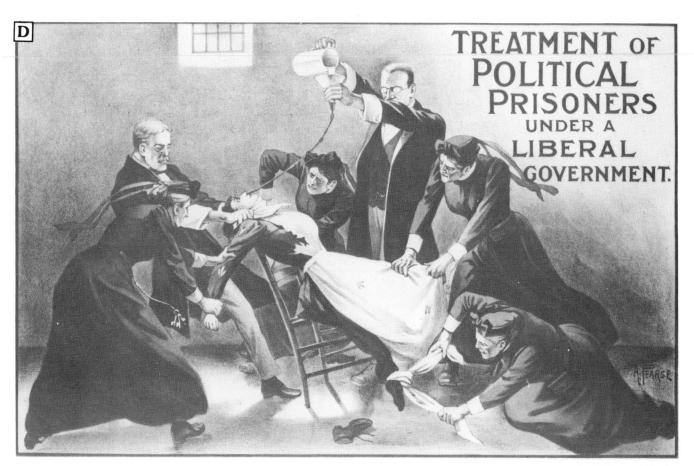

D TREATMENT OF POLITICAL PRISONERS UNDER A LIBERAL GOVERNMENT.

it said it could arrest them again when it liked. This was known as the *Cat and Mouse Act.*

The suffragettes demonstrated against the government's failure to give them the vote. Fighting was common at such demonstrations:

E *Policemen in uniform and plain clothes struck us in the chest, seized us by the arms and flung us to the ground. . . Two girls with linked arms were being dragged about by two uniformed officers. One of a group of officers in plain clothes ran up and kicked one of the girls, whilst the others laughed and jeered at her. . . The police snatched the flags, tore them to shreds, and smashed the sticks, or struck the women with fists and knees, knocked them down, some even kicked them, then dragged them up. . . witnesses and sufferers testified to deliberate acts of cruelty, such as twisting and wrenching of arms, wrists and thumbs. . . rubbing a woman's face against the railings. . . .*

When war broke out in 1914 the suffragettes stopped their protests. Most of them backed the war. Between 1914 and 1918 women took over many of the jobs done by men away fighting (see page 19). Their work in industry, agriculture and government showed that they were equal to men. After the war, in 1918, all women over 30 were given the vote.

? ? ? ? ? ? ? ? ? ? ? ?

1 a What is happening in **A**, **C** and **D**?
b What do these pictures tell us about the suffragettes?

2 Draw a poster from the Government's point of view to justify the forcible feeding of women suffragettes.

3 Tell the story in the picture from the viewpoint of *one* of the following people:
a the jockey or Emily Davison (picture **A**);
b the policeman holding Mrs Pankhurst, the suffragette leader (picture **C**);
c the suffragette or a woman warder (picture **D**).

4 Take the role of one of the people in **D** and say what your thoughts were about what you were doing: five minutes before the picture; at the time of the picture; when the forced feeding had ended.

5 What bias can you detect in **B**, **D** and **E**?

6 Interview two people, one over 60 and one between 30 and 40, about the ways in which women's roles have changed since they were at school. Also ask your teacher.

IMMIGRATION

A Number and origin of immigrants to Britain in 1981

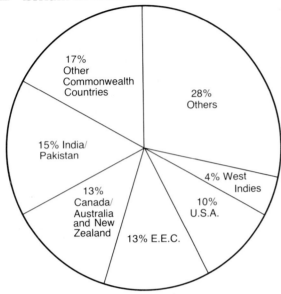

17%
Other
Commonwealth
Countries

28%
Others

15% India/
Pakistan

4% West
Indies

13%
Canada/
Australia
and New
Zealand

10%
U.S.A.

13% E.E.C.

Total immigrants: 174 000

B

'Wop', 'Yid', 'Mick', 'Pom', 'Jap' — all are terms of abuse used today to describe people from other countries. In the 1960s newspapers in Australia attacked settlers or *immigrants* from Britain. The newspapers said that the way they behaved was a disgrace, and that these 'Poms' should be sent home. For centuries settlers from other countries have come to Britain. All of us are descended from immigrants. Since 1900 many such people have come to live in Britain, **A** shows where the immigrants to Britain came from in 1981.

Before the First World War thousands of Jews arrived. They had escaped from Eastern Europe, where they would have been killed. In the 1930s many Germans fled to Britain from Hitler's Germany, and from 1938-45 people came from countries he conquered in Europe. During the 1950s began a large-scale immigration of coloured people to Britain, from the West Indies, India and Pakistan. These countries had been or were still part of the British Empire. Their inhabitants were British citizens. They came to England to fill jobs in the growing British economy. British firms and the British government advertised widely in the West Indies for workers to come to England. In the 1970s

Asians fled to Britain from Uganda, an African country. The Ugandan government forced them to leave. They came to Britain because Britain had ruled Uganda, and they were still British citizens.

Settlers from abroad often move into poor areas of Britain's cities, **B**. Where large numbers of immigrants live in one area of a city a *ghetto* might grow up, like the Indian one in Southall and the West Indian one in Brixton (both parts of London). Coloured immigrants mainly from Pakistan, India and the West Indies and their children who were born here often meet racial discrimination and abuse. They may even be attacked — just because their skins are not the same colour as that of their attackers. **C** is a story based on local newspaper accounts which tells of a racial conflict.

In 1958 there were race riots at Notting Hill in London. These riots seem to have been based on fear and ignorance. One newspaper, the *Daily Mirror*, tried to get some facts across to its readers, **D**.

C

YOUTH CLEARED OF ASSAULT

In court today Khalid Mahmood was cleared of a charge of assault, though found guilty of the lesser charge of carrying a dangerous weapon.

Khalid is 17, the eldest child of a large Asian family living in the mainly Asian area of the town. His four younger brothers are all deaf. The weekend before the incident Khalid's youngest brother Ghulum was sent to the shops. He was followed by a group of youths, described by the passers-by as skinheads. They asked him a number of questions, which, being deaf, he was unable to answer. ''They thought he was being cheeky, and threatened to hit him if he didn't answer,'' one eye-witness said. ''He just stood there looking confused, then they put the boot in.''

Despite there being over 30 witnesses, no one tried to intervene as the deaf, seven-year-old child was punched and kicked by about a dozen skinheads. ''I was scared to try and stop them — there were no Police around'' one man said. Ghulum was admitted to the general hospital where he needed 25 stitches.

The following weekend Khalid and a friend were jostled and insulted by another group of 'skinheads' at Woolworths. Khalid ran to the Police Station to ask for help, but the Police were not helpful. ''The skins had cleared off by now, but I knew they'd be back. The policeman said since there was no one around he could do nothing. He said 'I don't go looking for trouble'''

That evening when he went out Khalid took a kitchen knife with him. He and a friend were again met by the group of skinheads. Passers-by confirm that after being provoked and threatened Khalid pulled the knife and stabbed one of them. He was arrested but later released bound over to keep the peace. Michael Watts, the youth stabbed, was not seriously injured. He admitted in court to insulting Khalid, but denied attacking him. The stabbing was seen as self-defence.

A social worker commented, ''These incidents have ruined the work we were doing to bring black and white youths together''.

D

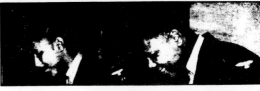

No. 1: INTRODUCING TO YOU...

They were born in Jamaica. Do you recognise the uniform?

THE BOYS FROM JAMAICA

● People are human beings even though they come in different colours. The main reason for race riots is plain IGNORANCE of this simple truth.

This is the first of a series which Keith Waterhouse is writing to give people the facts about the coloured people. Today — meet the Jamaicans:

Smiling Percival Bennett works on a co-operative farm in Jamaica.

❶ WHERE THEY COME FROM..

HALF the 200,000 coloured people in Britain come from the West Indies, a sunny chain of islands in the Caribbean, between North and South America.

About 70,000 of those are from Surrey, Middlesex and Cornwall—the three counties of Jamaica, British for 300 years.

By the cheapest route, it costs £75 for them to come to Britain—on a British passport.

Jamaicans have been leaving home to look for work since 1884. They helped to build the Panama Canal.

They emigrated to the U.S.A., to Cuba, to South America. After the war, they began to come here.

❷ WHAT THEY DO AT HOME..

JAMAICA makes the sunshine things. Sugar. Bananas. Coffee. Cocoa. Rum. Tobacco.

About half its workers are in these jobs. And about half its produce comes to Britain.

Jamaica exports £49,000,000 of goods a year. Yet unemployment is still one of its big problems.

To keep in world markets the country that desperately needs to create labour is obliged to import labour-saving machinery from Britain.

Jamaicans come here for jobs—but Jamaica helps to keep Britain in jobs. We make their machinery. And we provide 40 per cent of their imports.

❸ WHY THEY ARE HERE..

JAMAICA is the big-money island where jobs are few and pay is poor. The £30,000,000 bauxite industry employs fewer than 5,000 people.

The luxury tourist business, earning £10,000,000 a year, has jobs for only 5,700.

One out of every five Jamaican workers is permanently out of a job. And there is big seasonal unemployment among those who do have a job. Pay is as low as this: An unskilled hand in the cigar business earns £2 11s. 6d. for a fifty-three-hour week. A van driver gets £4 15s. A grade one railway fireman gets £5 10s.

Unemployment pay does not exist. The Jamaicans come here for work.

—WHEN WAR CAME...—

● During the war, 10,000 Jamaicans came voluntarily to this country to fight for Britain.
● Eight thousand of them went into the Armed Forces, and 2,000 into munitions work.

F A C T S

● ARE THEY WASTERS ? In three years, Jamaicans in Britain have sent home £10,000,000 in postal orders to their dependants

● ARE THEY CRIMINALS ? No Jamaican can leave the island without police clearance. Those with criminal records are not allowed to come.

● ARE THEY HEATHENS ? Three out of every five Jamaicans are members of a Christian church or group. In Britain, the churches they attend are packed.

● ARE THEY STEALING OUR WOMEN ? After the war, all the Jamaicans who came here were men. Nowadays, half of them are wives and children—coming to rejoin their husbands.

● ARE THEY STEALING OUR HOUSES ? Many Jamaicans here live in decrepit houses which white people would not take. Some have done renovations themselves.

● ARE THEY STEALING OUR JOBS ? Jamaicans today are in steel, coal, Lancashire cotton and public transport. Colour bar or no, there are still few jobs that employers will give to coloured people if they can get white workers instead.

Twenty-two per cent. of the Jamaicans coming to Britain were in white-collar jobs in the West Indies.

But only four per cent. can get office jobs here. Most become transport workers.

And that—according to West Indian welfare workers—accounts for the good manners of Jamaican bus conductors.

F A C T S

TOMORROW: Meet the West Africans...

???????????????????????????????????????

1 a Using **A**, list in order the countries and areas which immigrants came from in 1981. Put the largest number at the top, and lowest at the bottom.

b Copy out the points in **D** in your own words, with your thoughts about each point by its side. How have things changed since 1958?

2 Read **C** and answer the questions:

a Was the stabbing an act of revenge or self-defence?

b Why did the skinheads pick on the Pakistani lads?

c Would you have tried to stop the attack on the deaf boy?

d Is the newspaper account biased? If so, how?

e If you feel the police cannot help, is it right to arm yourself with a weapon?

f What could the social worker do to improve race relations in the area, after the attack?

THE ROYAL FAMILY

When you get home today you switch on the TV. A news flash appears on the screen:

A huge bomb has just gone off at Buckingham Palace. It is feared that the whole of the Royal Family has been killed. The Palace has been totally destroyed.

How would you feel? *Why* would you feel that way about the Royal Family?

Britain is one of the few countries still to have a King or Queen – a *monarchy*. **A** shows how the present Royal Family can trace its roots back to Queen Victoria, who was Queen in 1900.

On most days on TV and radio, or in the newspapers, there is a story about the Royal Family. This news makes me feel British – for we look to the Royal Family to show us the best side of British life.

The Queen and the Royal Family serve as a symbol of British life. This is shown clearly in times of war, when the Royal Family has led the fight against our national enemies. During World War I (1914-18) Prince Edward, the Prince of Wales, demanded to go and see the troops fighting in the trenches:

B *His presence was an enormous morale boost to the common soldier, he was popular everywhere he went among the men and his visits were looked forward to with great pleasure. Once he made a tour of the front at Vermelles. When he returned with his guides to their cars it was to find that they had been destroyed by shrapnel (a shell that explodes so that thousands of bits of its casing kill or wound people over a wide area) and that his chauffeur was dead.*

During the Second World War (1939-45) the King, Queen and Royal Family visited troops and areas the Germans had bombed, **C**.

D *During the morning the King and Queen saw a dozen scenes of devastation and were moved again by the amazing spirit with which*

A **The Royal family tree**

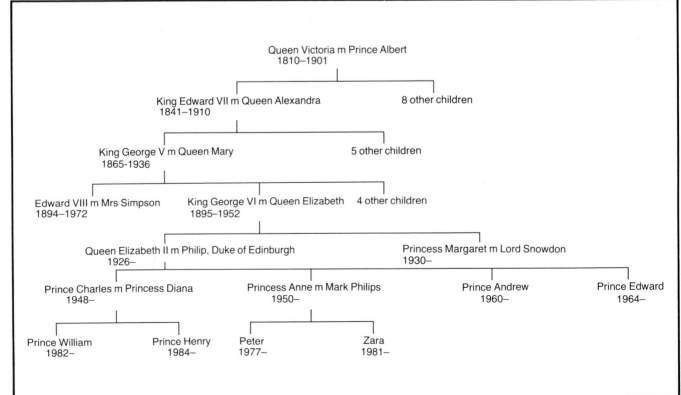

Queen Victoria m Prince Albert
1810–1901

King Edward VII m Queen Alexandra
1841–1910 — 8 other children

King George V m Queen Mary
1865-1936 — 5 other children

Edward VIII m Mrs Simpson
1894–1972

King George VI m Queen Elizabeth
1895–1952 — 4 other children

Queen Elizabeth II m Philip, Duke of Edinburgh
1926–

Princess Margaret m Lord Snowdon
1930–

Prince Charles m Princess Diana
1948–

Princess Anne m Mark Philips
1950–

Prince Andrew
1960–

Prince Edward
1964–

Prince William
1982–

Prince Henry
1984–

Peter
1977–

Zara
1981–

C

the common folk of London have responded to the German violence. As they came from a bomb crater on a spot where a block of workers' flats had stood, women pressed about them cheering, 'There'll always be an England.'

They climbed over great heaps of rubbish that had once been 12 small houses. Dust gathered thick upon the Queen's shoes and stockings. Here an elderly woman told her that her daughter and grandson had been killed. Another woman said to the Queen, 'Hitler can knock our houses down, but he can't get us down.'

Daily Herald, 12 September 1940

? ?

1 Bring to school or describe as many *signs* and *symbols* as you can find about the Royal Family *in the past* from:

Home: coronation mugs, tea towels, photographs. . .

School: portraits, house names. . .

In public: street names, monuments, statues, portraits, buildings, public houses. . .

2 Make out a table in date order showing the reigns of British kings and queens since 1900, using **A**. Match each piece of *evidence* **B-D** with one monarch or king and queen.

3 How might you have felt if you were a soldier:

   a At the front, **B**?

   b With the Prince of Wales on his return to his car, **B**?

   c When you were on duty in London and met the Queen, **C**?

   d If you saw the newsflash about the bomb?

4 Look at **C** and **D**. Imagine you lived in one of the houses before the bombs fell. Describe:

   a What life was like before the bombing.

   b The night of the bombing (Clues: air raid, shelter, rumours, morning, fires, firemen, home).

   c How you felt when you heard the Queen was coming.

   d What you said to the Queen.

   e What happened after she had gone, and your feelings about the Royal family.

ABDICATION!

Headlines something like this shocked the country in 1936, when the new King, Edward VIII, announced that he wanted to marry an American woman, Mrs Simpson. The problem was that Mrs Simpson was already married. To marry the King she would have to get a divorce. In fact Mr Simpson was her second husband; she had already been divorced once.

Divorce was still rare in the 1930s (see page 8). Many people disapproved of Mrs Simpson. The government, led by Prime Minister Stanley Baldwin, refused to allow the King to marry her. In November 1936 Mr Baldwin said:

A *The people of this country would never accept her as Queen. . . the Throne would be imperilled, the Empire would be endangered, there would be a demand for the King's abdication.*

The question of what the King should do was argued about in the newspapers, **B**. In

B

C

December the crisis ended when King Edward decided to *abdicate* (leave the throne) and marry Mrs Simpson, **C**. His brother became the new king, George VI. Edward said:

D *The decision has been made less difficult to me by the sure knowledge that my brother, with his long training in the public affairs of this country and with his fine qualities will be able to take my place forthwith without interruption or injury to the life and progress of the Empire.*

? ? ? ? ? ? ? ? ? ? ? ?

1 Who in **C** were: Mrs Simpson; the ex-King? What does the photograph tell you about them?

2 What might Mrs. Simpson's offer have been? What might the people in **B** have told you about their feelings towards Edward VIII?

3 In November 1936 which of these plans would you have advised Edward VIII to have followed:

    a marry Mrs Simpson and refuse to leave the throne

    b marry Mrs Simpson and get Parliament to agree that she would not be Queen and her children would not inherit the throne

    c live with Mrs Simpson and not marry her, and carry on as King

    d do nothing and wait for the government to act against the King

JUBILEE!

Who are the figures in **A**? When was the picture taken? Pictures **B** and **C** give some clues.

1977 was the 25th year of Queen Elizabeth II's rule. The whole country celebrated her Silver Jubilee with decorations – **B**, and street parties – **C**. The Duke of Edinburgh wrote:

D *People continue to have emotions of pride and attachment to their homeland. They still respond to symbolism more easily than to reason. The idea of chieftainship in its representative rather than in its governing function is still just as clearly and even instinctively understood. From the point of view of national identity this function is perhaps more important than ever. There is an obvious need for a symbol which helps to remind people that we are all citizens of the same country and that, in spite of differing political opinions and loyalties, we are still neighbours and need to be friends.*

(*The Daily Mirror*, 6 February 1977)

E shows just some of the jobs the Queen and the Royal Family have to do.

E

Open Parliament

Give her consent to Acts of Parliament

Make public visits to schools, factories, hospitals etc in Britain

Go on Royal tours to Commonwealth countries

Pay state visits to other countries

Be the Head of the Church of England

Act as leader of the Commonwealth

Set an example of good behaviour and family life for everyone to follow

? ? ? ? ? ? ? ? ? ? ? ?

1 a List the signs and symbols we use today, like stamps and coins, which show the Royal Family. What do they tell us about them?

b Keep a note for a week of the different things shown on TV and in the newspapers that the Royal Family do.

c Find out what the Queen does at: the Opening of Parliament; the Trooping of the Colour.

2 Put the points in **E** into what you think are their order of importance, and carry on with the following piece of writing:

I think the Royal Family is important because. . . .

3 Use **A** on page 24 to identify figures 1,2,3 and 4 in **A**. What jobs do they have today?

4 1977 was Silver Jubilee year. Who do you think organised each of the celebrations shown in **B-C**? What does this tell you about the Jubilee?

POLITICS

A suggests why politics matter to us all. Issues like the one in **A** affect all our lives — and politicians decide what to do about them. Since 1900 there have been huge changes in politics. One of the biggest has been the rise of the Labour Party. The Labour Party was formed in 1893. Before 1914 it did not get much support, but after the First World War (1914-18) it grew quickly. In 1919 all men got the vote. This helped Labour, as it relied upon working class support. Between 1919 and 1924 membership of the Labour party went up rapidly, **B**. Your local Labour party was most probably founded at this time. Labour began to replace the Liberal Party as the chief political party opposed to the Conservative Party, **C**.

By 1924 Labour Party support had grown so fast that Labour won the 1924 General Election. The Labour Party formed a government but it relied upon Liberal support and lasted only nine months. After the Second World War (1939-45) Labour won the 1945 general election with a majority of seats in Parliament. The Labour government stayed in power until 1951. From 1945-51 Labour pushed through many of its

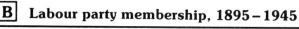

B Labour party membership, 1895–1945

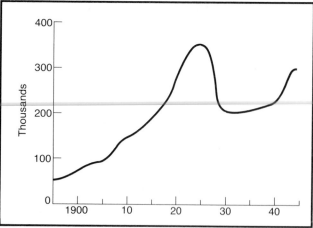

plans — see pages 32-33 — such as the take-over of British industries or *nationalisation*.

Between 1951 and 1984 Britain has been ruled by Labour and Conservative Governments, see **D**. In the 1950s the Conservatives carried on with many of Labour's plans. The 1950s saw a boom in the British economy. Most industries grew quickly, there were jobs for all and people were better off. The good times came to an end in the mid 1960s when the Labour government had to deal with an economic crisis which led to its fall in 1970. The Conservative government of 1970-74 faced many of the same problems, and lost the general election of 1974 mainly because it had been unable to deal successfully with a miners' strike.

The Labour government from 1974-79 also tried to solve the problem of the decline of British industry. It hoped to get trade unions and industry to work together. The failure of this plan, with the outbreak of strikes in the winter of 1978/79, meant that this government in turn

Then and Now.

LIBERAL PARTY: My dear sir, I am delighted to give you a lift. It is quite a pleasure to have your company.

LIBERAL PARTY: Dear me! If he grows much bigger, I shall be crowded out of the trap altogether.

It has been resolved that the Miners' Federation shall join the Labour Party.

was defeated in the 1979 General Election. In 1979 the Conservatives returned to office, under Britain's first woman Prime Minister, Mrs Margaret Thatcher.

Today Britain has four main political parties: Conservative, Labour, Liberal and SDP (Social Democratic Party). The Liberals and SDP stand jointly in local and national elections.

There have also been major changes in local government. Up to 1972 it was run along the lines set down in the 1880s and '90s, with county and county borough councils, and urban and rural district councils. These bodies were in charge of local services like schools, the workhouse and roads. In 1972 there was a huge shake-up and reorganisation of local government. Many of the old counties and boroughs (town councils) were swept away. New county and district authorities were set up in charge of local services, **E**.

D

Government	Dates	Prime Minister
Conservative	1951-64	Winston Churchill 1951-55 Anthony Eden 1955-57 Harold Macmillan 1957-63 Alec Douglas-Home 1963-64
Labour	1964-70	Harold Wilson 1964-70
Conservative	1970-74	Edward Heath 1970-74
Labour	1974-79	Harold Wilson 1974-76 James Callaghan 1976-79
Conservative	1979-	Margaret Thatcher 1979-

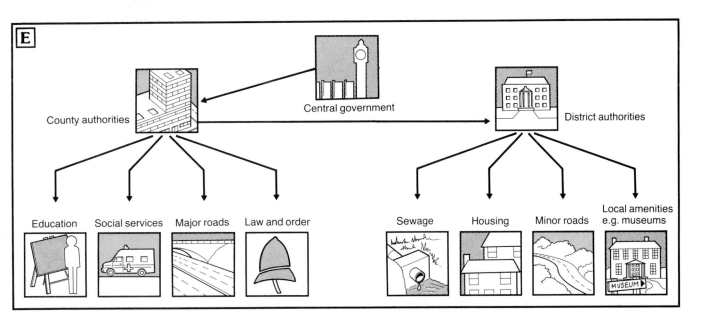

E

County authorities — Central government — District authorities

County authorities: Education, Social services, Major roads, Law and order

District authorities: Sewage, Housing, Minor roads, Local amenities e.g. museums

?????????????????????????????

1 How much do *you* know about politics?
a In **C**, who is sitting next to the man in the top hat?
b When might **C** have been drawn?
c When did the Liberals/ the Labour Party/ the Conservatives, last win a general election?
d When was Labour Party membership at its highest? Its lowest?

2 Look around your area for posters like **A**, about important local or national issues. Make out a questionnaire to find out what people in your school think about them.

3 What is wrong with your school? How would you like it to be run? Plan your own political party. How will it campaign to put things right? Think about organisation, membership, publicity, campaigns etc.

THE GENERAL STRIKE, 1926

A   *General Strike. Just used to get up. We had no soap. Just a bit of a wash. Of course they used to go to school. They had nothing to eat. Here's these little boys taking their bait bags, but for the love of God what they had in them I don't know. I've gone into a field many a time for my breakfast, a raw turnip. I've stole potatoes out of a heap. . . It's what we lived on. They don't know they're born today.*

B   *My father brought all the Lyons drivers out. . . But to me it was all wildly exciting and I helped to overturn trams driven by blacklegs at the Elephant and Castle. At the end of the strike my father lost his job and he found it hard to get another.* (He was not allowed to work as a newspaper van driver because he belonged to another union). *This was the only time we knew grinding poverty.*

The people who wrote **A** and **B** lived through the General Strike of 1926.

The strike began with the miners. The mine-owners were trying to make them work longer hours for less pay. The miners refused to accept this and came out on strike. On 3 May the TUC (Trades Union Congress) called on its members to support the miners and join in the strike. It

spread to workers on the railways and other transport services; in the printing, chemical and metal industries; iron and steel works; building and power stations.

The Government used volunteers, the army, navy and police force to keep vital industries going and break the strike, **C**, **D**. Sometimes fights broke out between the strikers and the 'blackleg' volunteers, **E**.

Volunteers unload paper supplies for an official newspaper

E

LATEST NEWS

LATEST STRIKE NEWS.

Miners Fed—On inquires late last night it was stated · that the Situation is unchanged.

Two Warships landed at Liverpool last night with food supplies.

The Police had some trouble at Poplar and Canning Town yesterday, gangs chiefly composed of youths made rushes near Poplar Hospital, a baton charge by the Police was necessary and several casualties were taken to Poplar Hospital, youths tried to prevent passengers on cars and one new car was destroyed. The Chief Commissioner states that the general position satisfactory throughout the country.

10,000 strikers out at Crewe.

Five cars overturned between Canal Bridge, Kinsland road and Liverpool street.

A few buses and lorrers have been stopped in parts of London and at Nottingham.

There has been some interferance, the situation is well in Hand and gives no cause for anxiety.

The Prime minister precided over a full Attendance To Day.

The Rumour that two Policemen Killed at Poplar is Denied.

The General Strike lasted nine days. Then the TUC told its members to go back to work. The miners still held out. But by November hunger (see **A**) forced them to accept defeat and return to work − on the mine-owners' terms.

Many people saw the General Strike as more than just a struggle over jobs:

F *Though some of (the volunteers) were recruited from the ranks of unemployed workers, the majority were ex-officers, medical students or Oxbridge undergraduates. Though the General Strike led to little bloodshed, and no deaths, it was still a class war.*

Some members of the Government had been afraid that Britain was on the brink of a revolution, like the one in Russia in 1917. They saw the collapse of the strike as a triumph of law, order and democracy over direct action by the unions. But many workers, especially the miners, were very bitter about it.

We still talk about the General Strike today. A historian made the points in **G**, about why it matters to us.

G

1 It was the closest Britain got to a revolution like the one in Russia in 1917.

2 It saw the end of the class war as an answer to Britain's problems.

3 It was a triumph of law, order and parliamentary democracy over direct action by the unions.

4 It led to the BBC being an independent body which could spread the news as well as the newspapers. In the General Strike the BBC had refused to do as the government told it.

5 It led to respect between workers and the upper and middle-classes, who had their first experience of manual work as volunteers.

？？？？？？？？？？？？

1 Looking at the evidence:
  a What were bait bags, **A**?
  b What was turnip used for, **A**?
  c What were blacklegs, **B**?
  d What were trams, **B**?
  e What was Lyons, **B**?
  f What was a baton charge, **E**?
  g What was the rumour in **E**?

2 a Who are the people in **D** and what are they doing?
  b Who are the people in **C**?

3 Look at the news in **E** and how it is written. What picture of the strike does it give? Do you think this is a biased view? Why?

4 If a General Strike like that of 1926 broke out where you lived, and you ran the local government, how would you deal with it? Draw up your plans. Mention:
  a use of police, troops, volunteers
  b power supplies − electric, gas, coal
  c food supplies
  d law and order − looting and rioting
  e news − radio, TV, newspapers
  f public services: education, local government, hospitals, medicine and health

5 Put the points in **G** in what you think are their order of importance for remembering the General Strike.

6 The writers of **A** and **B** were children in 1926. After the strike, what might their fathers have said and felt about: the Government; the TUC; the bosses?

LABOUR 1945-51

Western Europe is mostly on the verge of starvation. . . Everywhere there is indescribable confusion, mix-up of populations, destruction of dwelling houses, bridges and railway tracks, flooding of coal mines, shortage of every kind of necessity, and lack of transport to distribute even such goods as exist. In the Far East hundreds of thousands of people, if the reports are truthful, have been blown to fragments by atomic bombs. . . In India, Palestine, Persia, Egypt and other countries, troubles that the average person in England has not even heard of are just about ready to boil over.

It was August 1945. The Second World War was over. **A** talks about some of the problems abroad that faced the new Labour government and Prime Minister Clement Attlee, **B**. Labour had just fought a bitter election battle against Winston Churchill and the Conservatives.

At home, things were little better. Over a million new houses were needed straight away. Much

B

C Labour government nationalisation

1946	Bank of England
	Coal – National Coal Board set up to run mines
1947	Civil Aviation – by 1949 two publicly owned firms, BOAC and BEA, ran Britain's air transport industry
	Electricity – British Electricity Authority with twelve area boards
	Railways and road transport
1948	Gas – Gas Council with twelve area boards
1949	Iron and steel

of British industry was using old and inefficient machinery, and Britain had lost many of the foreign markets for her products. Many foodstuffs were still in short supply, and rationing became even stricter – bread was rationed in 1946. In addition, the winter of 1947 was the coldest of the century and there were widespread shortages of coal, electricity and food. Faced with these enormous difficulties, the Labour government began to push forward its

D The founding of the Welfare State

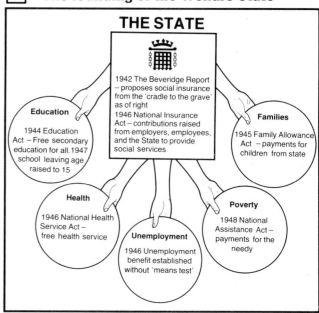

work for all... thanks to Labour

healthy thanks to Labour

THE GOOD NEIGHBOUR— VOTES LABOUR

HIS FUTURE— —YOUR VOTE! VOTE LABOUR

Family Allowances started 6th August 1946 by Labour

remember? UNEMPLOYMENT Don't give the Tories another chance VOTE LABOUR

KEEP IT GOING! VOTE FULL EMPLOYMENT LABOUR

They remember— and they're voting LABOUR

plans to rebuild British industry and reshape society.

In industry, Labour planned to *nationalise* many private concerns. The government took over many industries like coal, iron and steel, air transport, gas and electricity between 1946 and 1950, **C**. Since then, all governments have played an important part in deciding how industry should be run.

Labour had promised to give higher family allowances and old age pensions, to improve the health service, build more houses and create full employment. Between 1946 and 1950 the government set up the Welfare State, **D**, which is still in operation today.

E shows some of the posters Labour used in its election campaign in 1950.

In 1948 the Labour government gave India her Independence (freedom). The setting up of India and Pakistan (formed out of part of the old India) as independent countries led in the 1950s and '60s to the break up of the British Empire in Africa and Asia.

? ? ? ? ? ? ? ? ? ? ?

1 In your own words, list four of the problems that faced Britain in 1945, and put them in your order of importance.

2 Look at **C**. Which industries were nationalised between 1946 and 1949? What reasons can you suggest for why the Labour government might want to control any two of these industries?

3 Would the posters in **D** have persuaded you to vote Labour in 1950? Give reasons for your answer.

4 How important for Britain do you think was Labour's:
   a nationalising industry, mines and transport;
   b setting up the Welfare State (see pages 34-35);
   c giving India freedom?

THE WELFARE STATE

In 1900 a survey of York showed that two out of every five people were poor – that is, living in *poverty*. This meant that they could not afford healthy food; new clothes, heating or lighting; they did not have enough money for their rent and rates; they could not pay the doctor's and other bills.

The politician George Brown came from a poor family. He remembers what life was like when his father lost his job:

A *We were given tickets or vouchers which could be exchanged at a butcher's for little bits of meat. That was a shaming process. (His mother fell ill). Some body of officials – the old Poor Law Guardians, I suppose – had to accept that you were sufficiently in need for an ambulance to be sent. . . It was well into the next day before we could persuade anybody to send an ambulance for my mother. At last we did so and she went to hospital.*

This was the only time when we knew grinding poverty. We came under the old Poor Law of out-relief (help given to poor people who lived at home rather than in the workhouse, where they got in-relief). Every Friday I had to go to the workhouse with a little sack to collect our allotment of bread and treacle. I was bitterly

B **The long path to the Welfare State**

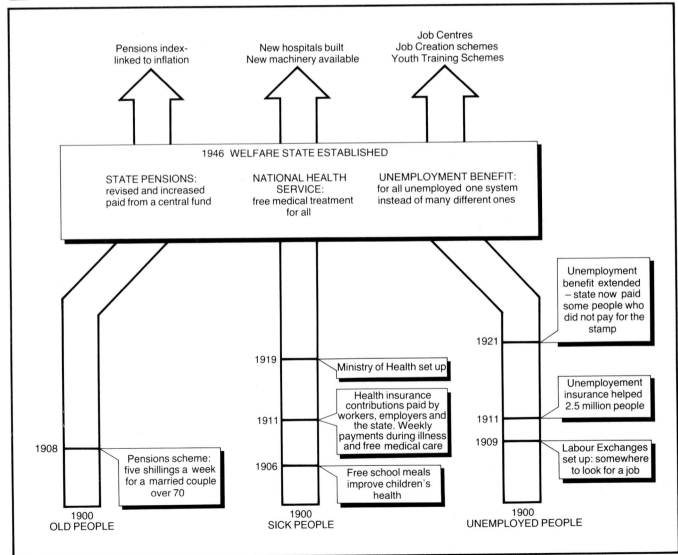

34

THE NEW YEAR'S GIFT.

From 1906-14 the Liberal government took steps to help the poor. It brought in Old Age Pensions in 1908, **C**, and set up *labour exchanges* (to help people find jobs) in 1909. In 1911 it passed the National Insurance Act (see pages 36-37) which helped people who were too ill to work, **D**.

During the Second World War (1939-45) the Government set up a group of experts, a committee, to look into poverty in Britain. The committee's head was Sir William Beveridge. Its findings were known as the *Beveridge Report*. After the war, the Labour Government acted on the report. Between 1946 and 1948 it passed Acts to help the poor, the sick and the unemployed (see pages 32-33) and founded the Welfare State. The Welfare State helped stamp out the grinding poverty that George Brown remembered (see **A**). But even today there are many poor families in Britain.

ashamed and bitterly angry. I swore then that I would do everything I could to see that people didn't have to take bags to the workhouse.

Many politicians were determined to get rid of poverty. But it was a long, hard struggle, **B**.

---

1 a What does **D** tell you about the National Insurance scheme of 1911?
b Who benefitted from the scheme?
c Why might some people dislike the 'Government line'?

2 What would happen to you in 1900, 1912 and today, if:
a you fell ill and could not work?
b you were aged 70 and out of work?
c you lost your job?

3 For each point below, say how George Brown, **A**, might have felt in 1926 when:
a he heard his father had lost his job;

b he was told he could only get enough food to eat if he applied for out-relief;
c he went with his sack to collect treacle and bread;
d he took tickets to the butcher for meat;
e he tried to get an ambulance to take his mother to hospital;
f his mother died.

4 Interview someone over 50 about life before the Welfare State and how things have changed since it was set up. Do you think people are better off since the Welfare State was set up?

MEDICINE AND HEALTH

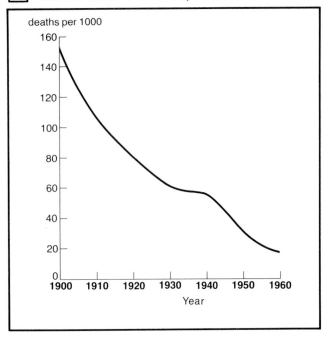

Look around your form. How many pupils are there? In 1900 about six of you would not have lived long enough to go to school at all. **A** shows how many babies died before the age of one.

Most babies in 1900 died from diseases which are now rare in Britain, such as typhoid fever and diphtheria. The high infant death rate in York in 1900 (see **A**) was due to an outbreak of influenza, typhoid fever and diarrhoea.

Today, we can take drugs to cure most of these illnesses. Many new drugs have been discovered since 1900. The most important is penicillin, which Alexander Fleming discovered in 1928.

We can also prevent illnesses by *inoculation*. The *vaccine* used gives you a mild form of the disease, and the body builds up its defences — so it can resist the real thing if it strikes. Since 1900 vaccines have been found for all the great killer diseases of the past century, **B**.

Today if you are ill you may go and see the doctor. In 1900 you would have had to pay for the visit. Most poor people could not afford doctors' fees. Sometimes they joined sick clubs or insurance schemes to help them pay. From a weekly wage of about 25s (£1.25) they would pay out 1-2s. Then, if they fell ill, the insurance scheme would pay them.

In 1911 the National Insurance Act was passed. This meant that the government would pay workers when they were ill. They could also get free medical care. But by 1939 the scheme only covered half the country. In 1948 the National Health Service replaced it. The NHS provided free medical care for everyone. This system is still in operation today — which is why you do not have to pay your doctor.

Standards of public health, hygiene and housing have improved a great deal since 1900. In 1901 a writer described one of the poorest areas of York:

C *A number of narrow and often sunless courts and alleys branch from these larger streets, and here it is that the poverty is chiefly found. . . Many of the yards and courts are unpaved, and brick ashpits and midden privies cleared only at rare intervals abound. . . There are 584 back-to-back houses in the district (one third). Of the 1642 houses, only 742 have private toilets. Of the remaining 900 the closets are used by two or more houses in common. Very many of the closets are in a most filthy condition. Less than half of the houses can boast a private water-tap. In some cases one water-tap is shared by over twenty houses.*

B New Vaccines

1796	Smallpox vaccine
1894	Diphtheria vaccine
1896	Typhoid vaccine
1905	Cholera vaccine
1906	Bubonic plague vaccine
1928	Yellow fever vaccine
1954	Polio vaccine
1965	Measles vaccine
1969	German measles vaccine

D shows a poor family from the East End of London in 1912.

Germs and diseases spread rapidly in these crowded and dirty conditions. **E** shows how conditions at home improved between 1951 and 1966.

E **Homes without basic amenities**

Amenity	1951	1966
No hot-water tap	No figure	13%
No fixed bath	37%	15%
No flush toilet	8%	2%

???????????????????????????

1 Look at **B**. When could babies in your area first be safe from: cholera; diphtheria; polio; typhoid; smallpox?

2 How would the following have been able
a to pay for a doctor
b have an operation for appendicitis in the years shown?

	1901	1912	1949
Unemployed miner Skilled carpenter Bank manager			

3 Imagine you are a doctor visiting home **D** in street **C**. Say what you: *see* as you enter the room (clues: light, water, toilets. . .); *smell*; *find* on the floor; *notice* about the children (hair, skin, clothes. . .). What suggestions would you make to the family about how to improve its health?

4 Put the following into what you think is their order of importance for good health:
Doctors/healthcare/hospitals
Health education
Vaccines
Medicines
Sanitation
Good nutrition

5 *Either*
a Explain the figures in table **A** *or*
b Describe the benefits of penicillin compared with other drugs.

SCHOOL

What sort of school do you go to – comprehensive, special, private, grammar, secondary modern? Why do they differ? In 1900 nine out of ten of you would have gone to a school like **A**.

Up to 1926 most pupils in state education went to a single school which they left at 14. Such schools were called *elementary* schools:

B *Our village school was poor and crowded, but in the end I relished it. It had a lovely reek of steaming life; boys' boots, girls' hair, stoves and sweat, blue ink, white chalk and shavings. We learnt just simple patterns of facts and letters, portable tricks of calculation, no more than was needed to measure a shed, write out a bill, read a swine-disease warning. Through the dead hours of the morning, through the long afternoons, we chanted away at our tables: 'Twelve inches one foot. Three foot makes a yard. Fourteen pounds make a stone.'* (from *Cider with Rosie* by Laurie Lee, 1959)

In 1926 a government report said that all children should go on to *secondary* schools at the age of 11, and stay there until at least 14. But by 1939 a third of the country's 11-year-olds were still being educated in the old 'all-age' schools.

Most parents had to pay to have their children educated at grammar school. Some children could win free scholarships, if they were clever. But going to the grammar school sometimes meant problems for poor scholarship children:

C *They lost the friends who had formerly been their classmates. When they came home in the afternoon they were supposed to do homework instead of rushing into the street to play.*

One London girl remembers:

D *The other kids made fun of us grammar school girls. They would shout out something about being stuck up or 'swank pot'. It was not just that they made fun of us, we just didn't have much in common.*

In 1944 parliament passed a new Education Act. It said that at 11 children should go to either a grammar or a secondary modern school. They had to take an examination called the 11-plus, to decide which they would go to. About three quarters of all children went to the secondary moderns. A teacher recalls:

E *. . . it was one of the most wonderful advances in education the country had seen. Even though you had reached school-leaving age you were encouraged to stay on. There's a girl in this town who is now a nurse. (She) was a C-stream girl. . . That girl stayed on at school, worked so hard, got three or four O-levels and became a district nurse. That was a thing completely unheard of in the past. It was a tremendous change. . . there were separate rooms for woodwork, metalwork, two rooms for housecraft, gym, labs, typewriters. . .*

During the 1950s many secondary modern and grammar schools were combined to form comprehensives, and new ones were built. Now nine out of ten pupils go to comprehensive schools, where they stay until the age of 16, or beyond, see **F**.

A

Date	State System	Private Sector
1900	Free education for the masses State elementary schools taught basic literacy and numeracy Education did not extend beyond elementary stage	Expensive education for the upper classes 'Public' schools for the privileged few. Small classes, good equipment. Former pupils reached the top in the Civil Service, professions and industry. Grammar schools (less expensive than the public schools) provided education for the middle classes.
1908	Grammar schools had to offer scholarships, giving free places to children from state elementary schools	
1914	1:40 pupils won a free place	
1918	Full-time education compulsory until 14	
1929	1:13 pupils won a free place at grammar school	
1944	**Butler's Education Act**. Good schooling now available to all classes. 3 types of free secondary school were set up: Grammar schools − for pupils who passed the 11-plus Secondary moderns − for those who failed the 11-plus Technical schools − for those good with their hands	Private education still an option for those who can afford it. But no longer the only entrance to a good career.
1947	School leaving age raised to 15	Many schools which had previously received money from the government now forced to become totally independent and raise fees.
1960s & '70s	Growth of comprehensive system. 11-plus examination abolished in many areas. All types of education now available to all	
1972	School leaving age raised to 16	

?????????????????????????????????

1 Match each head with its correct tail:

Head	Tail
You had to stay at school until you were 14	in the Butler Education Act of 1944
School leaving age was raised to 15	in 1947
In 1908 grammar schools had to offer free places	to give children of different abilities the same quality of education
Secondary modern schools began	in 1918
Comprehensive schools aimed	to enable children of high ability to have the best education

2 If you had gone to a school like **A**:
 a What would you have learnt by 14?
 b What use would it have been to you on leaving school?
 c How would your lessons have been different from what you are learning now?
 d How would you have been taught?
 e How was the secondary modern *better*, **E**?

3 Look at the classroom in **A**. How does it compare with your classroom? List **a** the similarities, **b** the differences.

4 What impact might being a grammar school pupil in 1955 have upon your links with old friends at junior school who went to the secondary modern − **C**, **D**?

SCHOOL
– LOCAL STUDY

You can find out a lot about the history of your school and of education in your area. The ideas below can help you start.

Written or Printed Sources

The local **Library** or **Record Office** may contain:

· *History books* about your region. Look in the Contents list and Index to see if there is any information on education.

· *Directories and guides*. These can tell you about the schools in your area.

· *Pictures and photographs*, **A**. (You might also find these in your own school.)

· *Maps*. The 25 inch and 6 inch Ordnance Survey maps show where schools were.

· *Local newspapers and magazines*. These may have articles or stories about your school.

· *Logbooks or diaries* from your school, **B**. These could well be in the Record Office or might still be at your school.

REMEMBER. When you visit a library always ask the Librarian to help you.

The **Local Education Authority** might have produced its own History of education in the area. To find out, you could write to the Chief Education Officer of your Local Education Authority.

Oral or Spoken Sources

People's **memories** about their schooldays can give you a lot of information. Copy out the questionnaire, **C**, or make up one of your own. Use the questionnaire to interview the oldest person you know, the longest-serving teacher at your school, your class teacher, the dinner ladies. . .

When you have completed the questionnaires, you can compare the answers under the different headings.

How are you going to present your results?

When you have collected all the information about your school and education in the area, you could present it in a number of ways. Here are just a few suggestions:

· as a wall display
· in a scrapbook
· as a History of education in the area
· as a play or pageant
· as a tape-recorded programme for local radio

When you have finished your local study and collected all your information, explain how you went about it. What has it taught you about how the historian works?

A

???????????

1 Look at **B**
  a What reasons are given for children being absent from school?
  b Why do you think some children were kept away in wet weather?
  c What lessons did the children have, according to the log book? What other things might they have been taught?

2 Keep a log book about your class for a week. What sorts of things will you record?

1901

22 Apr. The Rev. H. D. de Brisay visited.

23 " Edith Harvey (Junior Student) in school.

" " Reginald Orton is absent, as his sister is suffering from mumps.

26 " Criticism Lesson on "A Lifeboat" given by Annie Dennett (Senior Student) to Class I at 10.20 a.m. The Mistress of Method, Teacher of History, and some Senior Students present.

29 " Alice Bate (Senior Student) in school this week.

30 " The Rev. H. D. de Brisay visited.

May 6 Alice Bate in school.

" " Practice Lessons are being given this week by Senior Students, from 2.45-3.15 p.m.

7 " William Roper has returned.

8 " Several children are absent today owing to wet weather.

10 " Practice Lesson on "Flax" given by Nellie Jones (Senior Student) to Class I at 2.40 p.m. The Teacher of History present.

14 " Dorothy Smith has left, as her parents have removed from Summertown.

15 and — Tremenheere, Esq., Assistant Inspector

16 " of Training Colleges, and E. G. A. Holmes, Esq., H. M. I., visited to hear the following lessons given by Second Year Students:—

"The Lighthouse", Class I, by A. Dennett.
"The Mole", Class I, by E. Strickland.
"Writing 'es' on Dots", Class II, by F. Gibson.
The Principal and the Mistress of Method visited.

" A holiday was given in the afternoon of the 16th. (Ascension Day.)

17 The children were allowed to go at 11.30 a.m. in order to see the return of the Oxford Volunteers from South Africa.

" Reginald Orton is absent, as he is suffering from mumps.

20 Florence Cantwell (Senior Student) in school.

23 Gertrude Choldcroft is absent by order of the Medical Officer.

24 Closed school for the Whitsuntide Holidays, until Wednesday, May 29th.

29 Reopened school. B. Skerry absent for one day with leave.

C

QUESTIONNAIRE

This questionnaire must be shown to the person filling it in *before* you ask them the questions.

NAME_____

YEAR OF BIRTH_____

---

1 Where did you go to school (school's name, town, county)?

2 What kind of school was it (private/state)?

3 Between which dates did you go there?

4 If you moved to secondary school from your first school, what type of school was it?

5 When you were 14 (present third year), what lessons did you have?

6 What books did you use?

7 What did you write on and with?

8 What did you think of school?

9 How were these thoughts *different* from what you hoped for when you went to school?

10 What can you remember about the 11 plus examination?

11 What did you think of your teachers?

12 What punishments were there?

13 Did the teachers use radio, TV, pictures, films?

14 What was your most enjoyable subject? Why?

15 What was your least enjoyable subject?

16 What was a typical day like at school?

17 If you stayed at school until you were 16, say how your lessons changed from those when you were 14.

18 How did you travel to school?

19 Were there school meals? If not, what did you do for meals?

20 What stories can you remember about your school days?

21 Were they the happiest days of your life?

22 What can you remember of your relations with your teachers? Can you think of any stories about how you got on with them?

THE ECONOMY AND INDUSTRY

In 1870 Britain was the 'workshop of the world' – its richest industrial and trading nation. By 1900 the USA and Germany had overtaken Britain. The decline continued, becoming much sharper after the Second World War. Between 1945 and 1970 British industry grew slowly compared with other European countries. By the early 1970s she had fallen behind most of Europe, as well as the USA, Canada and Japan. Today, Britain is one of the poorest countries in Western Europe.

At the start of the century, Britain's industrial wealth still relied mainly on the industries which developed during the Industrial Revolution of 1750-1850 – industries like coal-mining, iron and steel, textiles and ship-building, see **A**. Often, family firms ran them, using old and well-tried, but sometimes outdated, methods and equipment. Since 1900 many of these older

A British industry at the start of the twentieth century

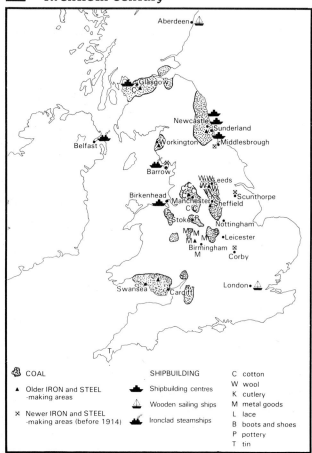

COAL

▲ Older IRON and STEEL -making areas

✕ Newer IRON and STEEL -making areas (before 1914)

SHIPBUILDING

⛴ Shipbuilding centres

⛵ Wooden sailing ships

🚢 Ironclad steamships

C cotton
W wool
K cutlery
M metal goods
L lace
B boots and shoes
P pottery
T tin

B Employment in coal-mining, 1955 – 1980

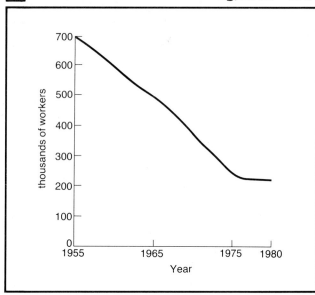

industries have gone into decline. Coal-mining and ship-building are typical.

A drop in demand for coal, and changes in how it is mined (see pages 46-47) has meant the closure of hundreds of pits. In 1948 there were 800 000 miners in Britain – today there are 120 000. The drop in numbers was sharpest in the 1960s, see **B**.

Ship-building has suffered in the same way. In 1900 Britain ranked first among the world's ship-building nations. In 1919 she was building seven out of every ten ships produced. By 1935

C Merchant ship-building, 1938 – 1970

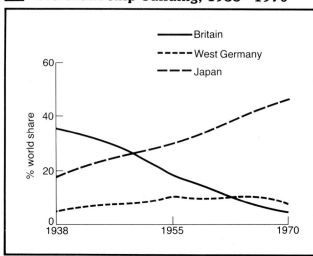

D Growth of new industries, 1900–1960

Electricity output	**1905**	533 million units
	1960	119 000 million units
Rubber production	**1900**	50 thousand tons
	1955	1 955 thousand tons
Refined petroleum	**1900**	150 million barrels
	1960	8 400 million barrels
Aluminium production	**1900**	9 thousand tons
	1957	3 310 thousand tons
Man-made fibres production	**1910**	3 thousand tons
	1957	2 427 thousand tons

this had become four in ten. Today, Britain builds only two ships in every hundred. During the 1930s, '40s and '50s other countries, particularly Japan and Germany, were developing new factory methods of ship-building. These were faster and cheaper than the old-fashioned methods used in British shipyards, which relied on skilled craftsmen and many unskilled workers. By 1956 Japan had taken the lead in the world's shipbuilding industry, **C**. Many British yards had to close down: in 1955 300 000 people were employed in British shipbuilding, today, there are around 70 000.

While older industries were running down, many new ones were growing up. **D** shows how new industries like chemicals, light engineering, electronics, motor car production, oil and gas, expanded rapidly between 1900 and the 1960s. Since the early 1970s, however, these newer industries have also begun to decline (see pages 46-47).

Between 1972 and 1980 rising *inflation* (the

E Inflation in the 1970s

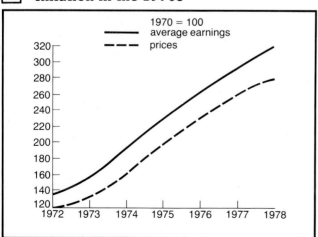

increase in prices) had a major impact on the British economy, **E**. As well as hitting industry, inflation affects all our lives. It means that people's wages do not stretch as far, and people who live on a fixed income (such as the Old Age Pension or unemployment benefit) are especially hard hit.

The state of the British economy is the subject of fierce debate in Parliament and elsewhere. Among the reasons put forward for Britain's industrial decline are:

· loss of markets after the collapse of the British Empire in Asia and Africa between 1948 and 1970
· failure of businessmen to invest their profits back into industry
· poor education of managers and workers
· the cost of fighting two World Wars
· 'wrecking tactics' of Trade Unions and militant workers
· the failure of governments to run the British economy properly
· lack of raw materials and resources
· the laziness of the British worker

? ? ? ? ? ? ? ? ? ? ? ?

1 Use **D** to work out how quickly the following industries grew. Put a tick in the right box:

	× 100	× 200	× 300	× 400
Electricity				
Aluminium				
Rubber				
Petroleum				

2 Choose three things you have at home (eg television, washing machine, computer) and try to find out where each was made. Was it in Britain? If not, why did your family decide to buy a foreign product, rather than one made at home? (Clues: price, reliability, appearance, durability)

3 Look at the list of reasons for the decline of British industry. Which ones do you agree with/disagree with? List them in your own order of importance.

THE DEPRESSION 1930-39

A Percentages of workers without a job in 1934

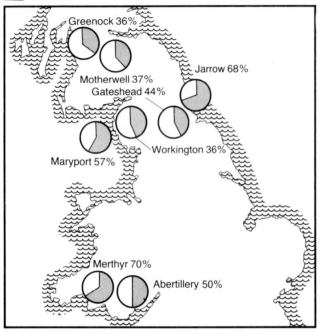

Greenock 36%
Jarrow 68%
Motherwell 37%
Gateshead 44%
Workington 36%
Maryport 57%
Merthyr 70%
Abertillery 50%

B Unemployment, 1928 – 1940

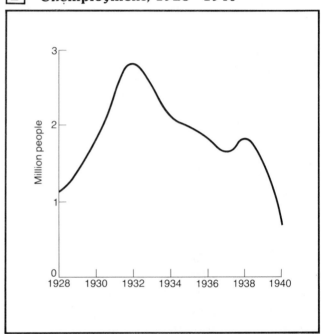

In the 1930s many British firms and factories were forced to close down, and thousands of jobs were lost, see **A** and **B**. The most badly hit industries were coal-mining, ship-building and textiles, the industries which had once made Britain the 'workshop of the world', (see p.42). The industrial collapse of the 1930s is known as 'The Depression'.

Ship-building towns like Jarrow, in County Durham, were very hard hit. When the ship-yards closed down thousands of men lost their jobs. By 1935 seven out of every ten workers in Jarrow were on the dole. The men were so desperate that they decided to march to London and demand Government help to find jobs, see **C**.

Memories of life in the 1930s are still fresh in many people's minds. The story of Edwin Routledge, of Wigton, Cumbria, is typical. Edwin started work as a miner, and then fought in the First World War (1914-18). After the war he worked as a miner in Yorkshire, and then returned to his home in Wigton. There he got a job in an artificial silk factory which used the buildings of an old jam factory:

44

E

making 'New-wrap', **E**, a sort of cellophane paper mainly used for wrapping cigarette packets. The factory opened in 1932 with four workers.

F *The factory as we know it started as British Newrap. I just went in as a labourer. I had to have a job of some kind and I was prepared to go in at the bottom of the ladder and prove what I could do when I got inside, see.*

A boom in house-building, for private buyers and for local government council housing, also meant a boost for British industry. It increased the demand for many manufactured goods, like bricks, glass, electrical cable and fittings, wood and paint. Gradually, Britain began to climb out of the depression.

D *The jam factory made jam for the troops in the First World War — then it changed to making sweets. But in the end it closed down, and it stood empty for years — and we got this artificial silk factory. It didn't last. The silk factory folded up. And then there was, from 1930 — from March 1930 until, well, in my case August 1933, practically no work at all. You got odd jobs here and there, but the unemployment in Wigton at that time was colossal, really, for a small town. The Labour Exchange was in Union Street, and I've seen them standing four deep — about half the length of Union Street — waiting to sign on.*

It was mostly the older industries that the depression hit. In the 1930s new sorts of industry grew quickly, such as car and radio manufacturing, chemicals and rayon. Edwin Routledge was able to get a job in a factory

??????????????

1 Why do you think:
a Edwin Routledge was unable to get a job (see **A** and **D**)?
b The artificial silk factory had to close, **D**?
c Britain began to come out of the depression?

2 What new industries would have been needed for the building of motor cars in the 1930s?

3 Imagine you are one of the men from Jarrow, in **C**. Write about what happened when the shipyards closed down and you decided to march to London. How did you feel on the march? What good did it do?

4 *Local study.* How has industry changed in your area since 1900? Visit your local reference library and look for:
· Trade and street directories, maps
· Local newspapers (look at articles, pictures, advertisements)
· Books on local history, collections of photographs

Make up a questionnaire and interview people in your area. When you have collected all the information, use it to make a scrapbook, class display, documentary or short drama.

BOOM AND SLUMP, 1951-80

After the Second World War (1939-45) British industry faced a crisis. George Orwell, a famous writer and journalist, wrote in 1945:

A   *We have lost most of our markets and overseas investments, twelve million tons of our shipping have gone to the bottom, much of our industry is hopelessly out of date and our coal mines are in such a state that for years it will be impossible to get enough coal out of them. We have ahead of us the enormous job of rebuilding industry and recapturing markets in the teeth of overwhelming competition from the USA.*

From 1945 to '51 British industry slowly began to recover from this crisis, although the Labour Government faced many problems (see pages 32-33). During the 1950s and '60s there was rapid economic growth. Economic growth meant jobs for almost everyone, high wages and the rapid expansion of new industries like television manufacture.

The town of Wigton (see p 44) benefited from the *boom* (rapid growth) like many others. By the 1970s most people were better off than they had been in the '50s. Edwin Routledge was still working for the 'Newrap' factory, see **B**. It had gone on growing in the 1940s and '50s, then:

C   *. . . in the Sixties it was taken over by SIDAC, an international and multi-national corporation which built a new factory cheek to cheek beside the old factory. Still, into the*

Seventies, the expansion goes on. I'm glad of the boom: I'm glad that people I know can move out of two-roomed damp gardenless slums into three-bedroomed council houses with bathrooms and lawns: I'm glad there is more money about for sweets and treats and holidays and clothes.*

Older industries like coal mining, ship building, iron and steel began to use machinery for jobs which used to be done by hand. This meant new ways of working. Changes like the ones in coal mining – see **D**-**G** – took place in many other industries. The writer George Orwell visited a mine in the 1940s:

D   *The first impression. . . is the frightful, deafening din from the conveyor belt which carries the coal away. You cannot see very far, because the fog of coal dust throws back the beam of your lamp, but you can see on either side of you the line of half-naked kneeling men, one to every four or five yards, driving their shovels under the fallen coal and flinging it swiftly over their left shoulder. It is a dreadful job that they do, an almost superhuman job. For they are not only shifting monstrous quantities of coal, they are also doing it in a position that doubles or trebles the work. . . Each man has to cut out, break up and load on the belt something between seven and twelve cubic yards of coal. That is to say that each man is shifting coal at a speed approaching two tons an hour.*

Things are very different in a modern mine, **E**. In 1972 Lord Robens, a past Chairman of the Coal Board (which ran the coal industry), wrote:

F   *In 1960 only 37.5% of the total output was power loaded – that is, it was cut and loaded on to conveyors by machines. Nevertheless, by the end of March 1964, almost three-quarters of the coal produced was mechanically cut and loaded. By 1970/71, 93% of all output was power loaded. . . Much of the hard slog has been taken over by the machines. The pick and shovel have become almost museum pieces on most coalfaces.*

E

The introduction of new machinery has meant a big drop in demand for unskilled and semi-skilled workers in many industries. The spread of robots and computers – a new 'Industrial Revolution' – has also reduced the number of workers needed.

Following the boom of the 1950s, '60s and early '70s there was a *slump* in the world economy, and this hit British industries badly. Mining was especially hard hit, as new sources of power were being found. The closing of many mines, **G**, has meant that miners have had to leave the industry or move to other areas to find work. Many have become unemployed.

While the older manufacturing industries have been declining there has been a big growth in the *service* industries, like teaching, catering and leisure. Today, fewer than three workers in ten are employed in manufacturing industry.

G **Number of coal mines, 1955 – 1980**

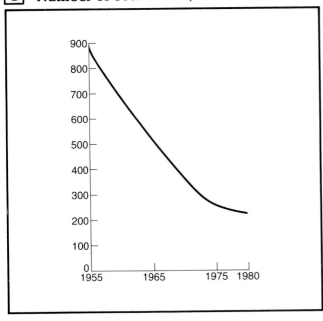

? ? ? ? ? ? ? ? ? ? ?

1 How has working in a coal mine changed since the 1950s (**D-F**)? Is it easier or harder today? What has happened to the number of people employed in mining?

2 What does **C** tell us about industry in the 1960s and early '70s? (Think about: number of jobs, work conditions, wages, effects on the community)

3 Can you think of any ways in which industry and work have changed during your lifetime? What sorts of jobs might you and your friends be doing in twenty years time?

TRANSPORT AND COMMUNICATIONS

A — Motor manufacture in Britain, 1923–1980

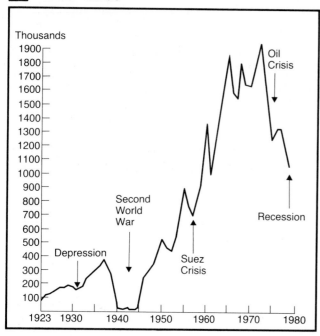

21 December 1900 Queen Victoria is woken up by her radio-alarm clock. After listening to the news she reads the daily papers. Then she has breakfast, watching morning TV. Afterwards she climbs into her mini and drives to the station. The royal train is due to leave at 10.00 for Heathrow, where she is catching a 'plane to America. At the airport she telephones Buckingham Palace. . .

How many mistakes can you spot?

Since 1900 there have been many changes in transport and communications, which have affected all our lives. The fastest form of transport in 1900 was the train. A network of railway track covered the country, reaching almost every town or large village. The railways were owned and run by 130 separate companies. These combined in 1923 to form four main companies: the London, Midland and Scottish Railway (L.M.S.); the Great Western Railway (G.W.R.); the London and North Eastern Railway (L.N.E.R.) and the Southern Railway (S.R.).

During the Second World War (1939-45) the government took over the railways. Then, in 1948, they were nationalised by the Labour government. In 1955 diesel engines began to replace the old steam locomotives.

By this time the railways were under threat from a rival form of transport – the motor car. In 1913 William Morris began making Britain's first mass-produced cars at his factory in Cowley, near Oxford. Mass production meant that cars could be built much more quickly and cheaply. Lorries and buses replaced horse transport for passengers and goods. In the 1920s and '30s the motor industry grew rapidly in centres like Cowley and Birmingham. Growth continued through the '40s and '50s, see **A**.

By 1960 most families owned a car. A system of motorways spread across the country, **B**. The railways could not compete. They were losing so much money that drastic action had to be

B — Britain's motorway network

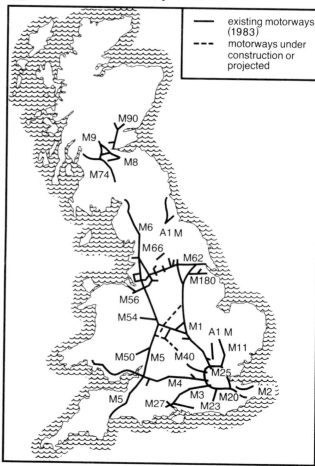

48

taken. In 1963 Dr Beeching, the Minister in charge of the railways, put forward a plan to *axe* (close down) 5000 miles of loss-making track. By 1970, 7000 miles of track had gone. Only main lines, plus a few 'feeders', survived, **C**.

In 1900 the idea of flying was just a dream for most people. Yet today many of us can expect to travel by air, for business or on holiday. Jet travel has opened up the world for ordinary people in the last 30 years. Low air fares have made holidays abroad almost as cheap as holidays in Britain. We can travel 1000 miles in a jet 'plane like Concorde in less time than the Victorians took to travel 100 miles, **D**.

Since 1900 telephone, radio and television have revolutionized communications. The telephone was invented in the 1870s. Today, just over 100 years later, it is a vital part of everyday life for many people. It allows them to talk to business colleagues, friends or family in the next street – or in Australia!

The first radio signals were sent at the end of the nineteenth century. In 1939, an article in a transport magazine said:

E *. . . from the early experiments of the sending of wireless signals a world-wide system*

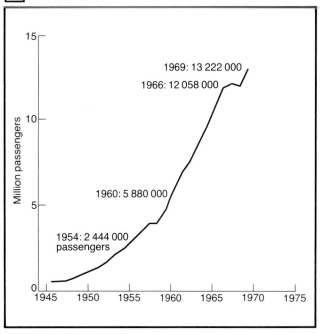

1969: 13 222 000
1966: 12 058 000
1960: 5 880 000
1954: 2 444 000 passengers

has grown whereby the earth has been encircled by an extensive network of wireless services. . . It may even happen that in years to come telegrams may be projected through space. . .

Television followed radio. In 1962 Telstar, the first satellite for relaying TV signals, was launched. This made it possible to watch live television across the world. In 1969 millions of people watched man's first steps on the moon. Today, we can watch events as they happen all over the world, or record them on video machines to watch when we choose.

C **Main railways in Britain**

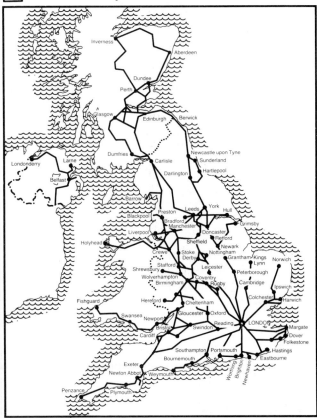

1 How many errors did you spot in the first paragraph? What were they? How do you think Queen Victoria would really have set out on a journey?

2 Interview someone over 40 about changes in transport and communications. Ask them about when they first had: a car, a TV, radio, telephone. . . How did it change family life?

3 What changes in transport and communications can *you* remember? How have they affected your life?

4 How do you think transport and communications will have changed by the year 2001?

49

BRITAIN AT WAR

Next time you walk around a village or town, look out for war memorials in churches or public squares. War memorials can tell us a lot about the impact of a war upon a place. How many men were killed? How many families did they belong to? How many men from the same family died? Most war memorials commemorate the men who died in the First World War (1914-18) and the Second World War (1939-45). But since 1900 British troops have fought in many battles all over the world, **A**.

In 1900 British forces were fighting a bitter war, the Boer War, to gain control over an area in southern Africa. The British were fighting the Boers, Dutch settlers in South Africa. The Boers had settled in South Africa before the British took over, and in 1900 wanted to be free to run their own country.

Since 1900 people in many of Britain's other colonies have struggled to win their freedom from the British Empire. In the 1950s and '60s this led to many bitter wars in Africa and Asia. In 1982 Britain and Argentina went to war over the Falkland Islands, a British colony off the tip of South America.

Local newspapers are a good source of facts about the impact of war upon the area where you live. Evidence **B**-**G** comes from copies of Exeter's newspaper, published in July 1917.

Many people can remember what life was like during the Second World War. The writer of **H** tells us how the real meaning of war was brought home to him in 1943, when he was a schoolboy.

H *And the deserted churchyard (where we played at soldiers) was full of slime-stained jam jars. Lobbed like Mills bombs they exploded with a satisfying crash against weeping angels and broken columns. It was young Fred Guest who stopped us. Old Fred, his grandfather, looked after the church itself and the roses which half-bloomed along the path. . . Young Fred was wounded in North Africa. Whilst the holes healed, Canon George Cherry Weaver, M.A. (Oxon), gave him cigarette money in return for*

A Some wars involving British forces, 1899 – 1982

Dates	War
1899-1902	**Boer War** South Africa. 400 000 British troops fought the Boers, the descendants of Dutch settlers.
1914-18	**First World War** Britain, France and Russia fought Germany and Austria-Hungary. The war was fought mainly in the trenches in France and Belgium (Western Front) and in Russia (Eastern Front). **1917** The Russians were defeated. America joined the Allies. **1918** Russia signed a peace treaty. The Germans mounted a massive attack on the Allies. The Allies held out, then counter attacked. Germany was defeated. Peace was declared in November.
1939-45	**Second World War** **1939** 1 Sept Germany invaded Poland. 3 Sept Britain and France declared war on Germany. **1940** Germany invaded Norway, Denmark, Belgium, Holland, Luxembourg, France. British troops evacuated from Dunkirk. **1941** Germany invaded Russia. Japan attacked American base at Pearl Harbour, leading to war in the Pacific. **1942-43** Germany fought the Allies in North Africa, and was defeated – at El Alamein. Germany defeated in Russia. **1944** 6 June – 'D-Day' – Allies invaded Europe. **1945** Germany surrendered. 6 Aug atom bomb dropped on Hiroshima – Japan surrendered.
1950-53	**Korean War** United Nations forces (including British) fought against the Communists in Korea.
1952-56	**Mau Mau uprising** British troops fought the Mau Mau terrorist freedom fighters in Kenya.
1956	**Suez Crisis** British and French forces fought the Egyptians over control of the Suez Canal.
1958	**Cyprus campaign** British fought against terrorists/freedom fighters
1982	**Falklands War** British forces fought Argentinians over possession of the Falkland Islands in the South Atlantic.

the removal of the twitch grass and willow herb. Suddenly there was a real soldier wounded in a real war to talk to. We carried his scythe, dragged away the cut grass and talked about the motor-bike he would buy after the war. As he grew stronger he helped dig the new graves and we sat and watched. Ten days after he left Sheffield, somebody dug a grave for him at Anzio. That death was more real to us than all the war that had gone before. . . Having known a man shot dead by one of Hitler's bullets was real. It made it impossible to play at war again.'

B
FOOD CONCESSIONS
respecting Butchers' Meat, Bacon and Ham

The food controller has issued an order which comes into effect on and from tomorrow, by which all bacon may be sold free of coupons. Holders of ration books are not permitted to change their dealer. . . Not less than 8 ounces of bacon, or 12 ounces of ham, are to be supplied per week per customer if demanded.

C
St Thomas (East)
War Weapons Week

Below is a list of the parishes in St. Thomas' East Area which took part in the War Weapons Week Campaign from July 13th to 20th, together with the amount raised in each case. . . Silverton over £10 per head. . .

D
SOLDIERS AND CHRISTIANS
Newton Abbot Tailor and His Conscience

James Hancock, Tailor, 32, applied on conscientious grounds and said that for thirty years it had been his conviction that he would not, as a Christian, become a soldier, and he could not engage in military training, or be armed with any weapon for the taking of human life, as it would be inconsistent, as a Christian, for him to do so.
Mr G. D. Woolacombe: '*Are you willing to undertake other work of national importance?*'
Hancock: '*My present position is a certified one – wholesale tailoring*'
. . . Hancock said he had no objection to doing ambulance work
Major Oswald-Brown: '*I should hope not, good Lord!*'

E
FOR TOMMY AND JACK
Scheme to Provide Land on Return to Their Former Homes

With the object of enabling discharged soldiers from country parishes on their return to their former homes to obtain a piece of land for cultivation on a voluntary basis, a scheme has been devised by the Central Land Association. (The land to be) plots or a little field of five acres or thereabouts close to the cottage in which the demobilised soldier or sailor lives.

F
ROLL OF HONOUR
West-Country Casualties in Recent Fighting

Pte. F. Parson (Exeter) Middlesex Regiment, is officially reported to have died of wounds; L. J. Brealy (Bovey Tracey), Wiltshire Regiment, and Lance-Corpl. N. F. Mardon (Dartmouth) Worcester Regiment, to be wounded Mr. A. Bellringer, of 32, Radford-road, Exeter, has received a post card from the Red Cross Order of St. John stating that his son, Private F. C. Bellringer, 2nd. Devon, is a prisoner of war in Germany and is well. He was reported missing on May 25th last.

G
Why Fruit Stones and Nut Shells are Wanted

Fruit stones and hard nutshells are urgently demanded by the Government for conversion into charcoal, which is to be used in the British respirator for the protection of our troops against poison gas. The urgency of the need will be seen from the fact that at present no other substance is known to give equal protection.

---

1 Use **A** to mark on a map where Britain has fought her main wars since 1900. What reasons can you suggest for why they were fought in these places?

2 Match clues **B-G** with the ideas below:
· raising money for weapons
· helping in the 'war effort' to provide better equipment
· keeping spirits up
· the impact of war on local families
· making men fight
· plans for the troops after the war

3 Make up and act out a short drama about the story in **H** – the schoolboys playing at war, making friends with Young Fred. How do they react when Old Fred tells them of his grandson's death?

4 Find out as much as you can about the Falklands War (use interviews, newspapers, books and anything else you can find). When did it start? Why was it fought? Who was involved? What was the outcome? How might an Argentinian of your age feel about Britain and the Falklands?

THE TRENCHES

Do you ever have nightmares? Have you ever felt really afraid, sick, or horrified by things you have seen or heard — either in real life or on the radio or TV? About 70 years ago your great-grandfather or his father, and his friends might well have lived through such horrors. They would have fought in the *trenches* in France in The First World War.

Since 1900 British troops have fought in many wars. The two biggest were the First World War, 1914-18 and the Second World War, 1939-45. From 1914-18 Britain, France, Italy and America (the *Allies*) fought Germany and Austria-Hungary. The British army mainly fought in France. Most of the fighting was done in the trenches. Your great-grandfather may well have fought in battles like the Somme, in July 1916. The Somme was like most other battles on the Western Front. Both sides had dug themselves a system of trenches, see **A** and **B**. From these the British and German troops faced each other across an area of barbed wire and churned up mud, full of water-filled shell holes, **C**. This was called *No Man's Land*. Behind the front trenches ran a network of more trenches, each with thick defences.

In the battle heavy British guns would bombard the German trenches. Then, on the order to attack, British troops would swarm over the top in thousands, **D**. A few British might capture some enemy trenches:

A How a trench was constructed

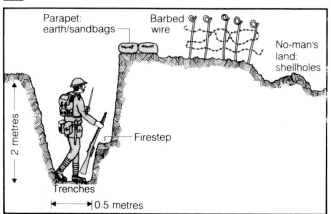

Parapet: earth/sandbags — Barbed wire — No-man's land: shellholes — 2 metres — Firestep — Trenches — 0.5 metres

B The British trench system

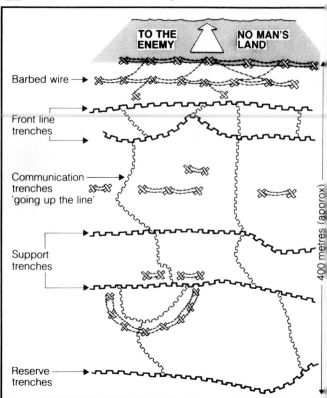

TO THE ENEMY — NO MAN'S LAND
Barbed wire →
Front line trenches →
Communication trenches 'going up the line' →
Support trenches →
Reserve trenches →
400 metres (approx)

E   *As I stepped over one of the Germans an impulse made me lift him up from the miserable ditch. Propped against the bank, his blond face was undisfigured, except by the mud which I wiped from his eyes and mouth with my coat sleeve. He'd evidently been killed while digging, for his tunic was knotted loosely about his shoulders. He didn't look to be more than eighteen. Hoisting him a little higher, I thought what a gentle face he had. . .*

C

Being in an exploring frame of mind, I took a bag of bombs and crawled another sixty or seventy yards with Kendle close behind me. . . From the other side of the valley came an occasional rifle shot, and a helmet bobbed up for a moment. I felt adventurous and it seemed as if Kendle and I were having great fun together. Kendle thought so too. The helmet bobbed up again. "I'll just have a shot at him," he said. . . I remember seeing him push his tin hat back from his forehead and then raise himself to take aim. After firing once he looked at us with a lively smile. A second later he fell sideways. A blotchy mark showed where the bullet had hit him just above the eyes. (Siegfried Sassoon)

??????????????????????????????

1 Split into pairs. One of you shuts your eyes, the other leads the person with shut eyes around the school. Change roles for returning to the classroom. Then say how a blinded soldier might have felt in the 24 hours after being blinded.

2 Look at **C**. You are a British officer standing next to the photographer. You have been ordered to go and help men trapped inside the tank who are under fire. You are in full view of German snipers. Plan out how you will get there, the orders you will give to your men left in the trenches, and how you might feel on reaching the tank safely. What will you do next?

3 Look at evidence **A-E**. Imagine you are Kendle's mother or father. How do you react when:

a War is declared on Germany?
b Kendle is called up, trained, and comes home on leave just before going to France?
c You get letters from him (censored) which tell you about life in the trenches? (Clues: lice, fleas, unwashed, wet all day, muddy, fear.)
d You hear of his death?
e Sassoon visits you to tell you how Kendle died and how they lived in the trenches?

4 What might have happened to the men in **D**: five minutes; one hour; after the photograph was taken?

5 *Local Study.* Find war monuments in local churches and public places. What do they tell you about the war's impact? Look at old copies of local newspapers to see how it affected people. Try and read the War Poets and memoirs of men like Siegfried Sassoon, Robert Graves, Wilfred Owen, Edmund Blunden.

THE SECOND WORLD WAR

In 1919 many Germans were bitter at defeat. They hated the terms of the peace treaty the Allies forced upon Germany. Germany lost much land; most of her army; her navy and her colonies abroad. She was forced to accept that she was guilty for causing the war, and she had to pay huge amounts of money to the Allies to pay for her 'war guilt' and the damage she had caused.

One German in particular thirsted for revenge – Adolf Hitler. In the 1920s Hitler built up his Nazi party. In 1933 Hitler became ruler of Germany. The Nazi party got Germany's army and navy ready to win back the lands in Europe which were lost in 1919. Hitler believed that the Germans were a master race of pure *Aryan* blood. Germany would wipe out 'impure' races like Jews, Gypsies and Negroes. Also, she would conquer the Slavs of Eastern Europe – the Poles and Russians. German settlers would take over their land.

In 1939 war broke out again in Europe, between Germany and Britain and France. Hitler had invaded Poland, and on 3 September 1939 Britain and France declared war on Germany. They had promised to defend Poland. The Second World War had begun.

This time the fighting was unlike that of 1914-18. Everyone was involved in the struggle. Both sides used aircraft to drop bombs on towns and cities, killing and injuring thousands of people. On pages 56-57 you can find out how the war was fought on the 'home front'.

In July 1940 Britain was in great danger. The Germans had defeated the French and routed the British army in France. The British army had been pushed back to the coast. Thousands of men were stranded on the beaches of Dunkirk, in Normandy. A fleet of small boats crossed the channel to rescue the stranded soldiers.

With the British army out of the way Hitler could concentrate on Operation Sealion, his plan to invade Britain. The first stage was to win control of the air. From July to September the Luftwaffe (the German air force) sent waves of aircraft over to Britain. Each time the attacks were beaten off by the Royal Air Force – which had only a few hundred trained pilots. This became known as the Battle of Britain. Winston Churchill, the British Prime Minister, said:

A   *Never in the field of human conflict was so much owed by so many to so few.*

Hitler was forced to put off his invasion. Instead, he turned to another form of attack: air raids. The *Blitz* began on 7 September 1940. It went on until the summer of 1941, and by the end 2½ million people in Britain were homeless and 43 000 had been killed. To escape the bombing, thousands of city children were *evacuated* (sent away to the country). **B-E** are evidence of what happened during the Blitz.

B   *The Sheffield Blitz did not take us by surprise. Coventry had been hit in early December (1940). . . It could only be a matter of time before the Luftwaffe moved its blitzkrieg north to the industrial cities of Yorkshire. Our chosen days were Thursday and Sunday the 12th and 15th of December. The factories escaped but the city centre was flattened.*

C   *On the first night we simply sat on the living room floor and waited for it to be over. My grandmother, an invalid, was incapable of taking refuge in a real shelter. The beams of her bedroom floor above her head were strengthened by steel girders that ran along the living-room ceiling. Four steel columns held the girders in place. My mother cried a little when they chipped away the plaster to take the ends of the girders. I fell into the hole cut in the floorboards to let the tent poles through.*

D   *The Luftwaffe came in waves. First we would hear their engines, then anti-aircraft fire, then the dull distant thuds as the bombs fell on Marple's public house, Foster's store and the Castle Street Co-op. Joey, an elderly budgerigar, seemed to have the gift of prophecy or very good hearing. Every time he rang his bell we* *knew that the cycle — engines, guns, bombs — was about to begin again. There was some talk of strangling Joey. But we all survived the night. I was forbidden to crawl into the front room and see the red glow over Sheffield, wept about it a little and fell asleep before the 'All Clear' sounded.*

(from *Goodbye to Yorkshire* by Roy Hattersley)

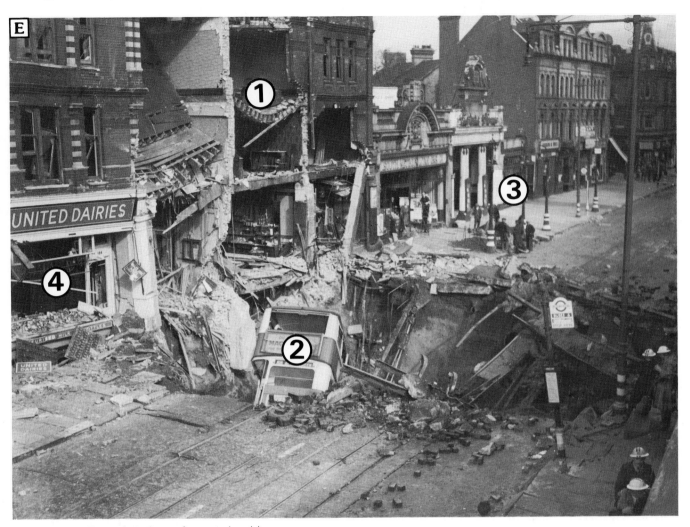

A street in Balham, London, after an air raid

1 Aryans have fair hair and blue eyes. What would the Germans have done to members of your form *without* these Aryan features?

2 a What can you see at points **1-4** on picture **E**?
b What does **D** tell you about the Blitz and its impact on British towns?

3 If you had been a friend of the schoolboy in **D** and you had visited his house on the night of the Sheffield Blitz, say what it might have been like to be there. Mention: playing; supper; the living room; dark; Joey; sirens; bombers; bombs; talk; curtains; fears; fire-watchers; all-clear.

4 Find out as much as you can about Dunkirk, the Battle of Britain and the Blitz by talking to people over 50 years old or going to your school and local libraries. Use what you find out to make up a radio programme about Dunkirk or the Battle of Britain or the Blitz.

5 Things to talk about:
a Why is Dunkirk talked about today as if it was a British victory?
b What would have happened to Britain if Hitler had invaded and won the war?
c What did Churchill mean by statement **A**?

THE HOME FRONT

From 1939 the British Government could tell people where to live and what jobs to do. The government rationed food and clothes, kept a tight control over the news and tried to make sure that everyone played an active part in the 'war effort'. **A-F** are clues about how the Second World War changed the lives of people who are now aged over 40.

Rationing

Food was rationed after January 1940. Every family was issued with a ration book. This allowed them to buy a set amount of certain kinds of food each week, **A**. Some foods, like fish, milk, bread and potatoes, were sold at fixed prices. Short supplies meant that people had to queue for hours to buy food. The 'Dig for Victory' campaign encouraged people to grow their own vegetables, **B**. Another way round rationing was to buy food illegally on the 'black market'.

Civil Defence

The Government believed that the Germans might use poison gas, as they had done in the First World War. Everyone was issued with a gas mask, **C**, which had to be carried at all times.

All men who were not fighting in the armed forces had jobs to do to help win the war. They would either be air-raid wardens, policemen, firewatchers, or members of the Home Guard. Every street had its firewatchers. What did this mean for school children?

D　*Sheffield, Yorkshire. I soon learned that for people like us, duty meant firewatching. They were two busy years (1940-41) for firewatchers. Most nights there was a raid of sorts – a false alarm, a single incendiary bomb in a neighbour's garden. . .*

After the fall of France in 1940, many people thought that Hitler would invade at any minute. A civil defence force – the Home Guard – was set up, **E**. Even children's books were infected by the fear of invasion.

F　*Mole "Hare! You shall be the Home Guard! You must defend Grey Rabbit's house and all our homes with your life. . . Squirrel, you must knit socks and stockings and mittens*

A		
1 185 grammes	liquid milk
225 grammes	sugar
55 grammes	coffee
85 grammes	cheese
115 grammes	jam
225 grammes	fat
Just over ½ an egg	
1s 2d worth of meat	
Unrestricted: bread, cereals & potatoes.	

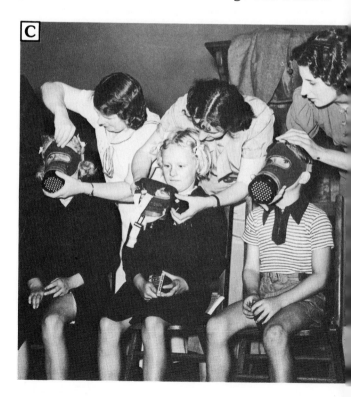

and scarves for all our fighters. Grey Rabbit! You must be a nurse and take care of the wounded."
Hedgehog "What about me? I may be old but I can fight. I once killed an adder with my prickles."
Mole "You are a brave fellow, Hedgehog, I shall want you to be a leader, a captain. Water Rat will guard the river banks. Wise Owl will fly over the woods and watch for the approach of the enemy. All the rest of the animals will be fighters, hidden on the war-path with bows and arrows, with pop-guns and swords and daggers. I shall dig a cavern underground where the young ones can hide in safety."
. . . (An army of weasels was marching along the old grass-covered Roman road.) Their leader said: "Grey Rabbit lives over there, Hare and Squirrel with her. We will eat them all up and live in their house. Then we will eat all the rabbits and squirrels and hedgehogs and mice in the country. They are kind, gentle animals and they will never dare to resist us".

Women at Work

Women took over a huge range of jobs which men had done before. They drove lorries, buses and ambulances. They worked on farms to increase Britain's food production, or in factories making weapons, ammunition, aircraft, and other vital supplies.

??????????????

1 Use **A** to plan a week's menu. How does it compare with the meals you eat now?

2 For *one* of pictures **B**, **C**, **E**, write down:
   a what the people are doing
   b what they might be thinking about
   c how the war might have changed their lives

3 Make a list of the things the animals in **F** decide to do. What does this tell you about the way people joined in the war effort? What do you think happened next in the story?

4 Take on the role of one of the people on this page. Ask your friends to take on different roles. Imagine you are all passengers on a bus in 1940. Last night the town was heavily bombed; some people think German paratroopers landed. . . Now continue the conversation between the passengers.

5 Interview someone over 50 about the Second World War. (Use a tape-recorder if you can.) Ask them about: the start of the war, gas masks, blackout, evacuation, rationing, the Blitz, air raid wardens, Dunkirk, D-Day.

CHURCHILL

During the 1930s Winston Churchill and a few supporters warned against the growing Nazi menace to Britain. Churchill said Hitler aimed to conquer Europe and carry out his plans for the German master race. In 1939 war broke out — see pages 54-55.

By May 1940 the Germans had overrun Poland, Belgium, Holland, Luxembourg, France and Norway. It seemed that Churchill had been right in the 1930s. The British Prime Minister, Neville Chamberlain, resigned on 10 May. The public wanted Churchill to lead the fight against the Germans. Already he was running the navy. Churchill became the new Prime Minister. He said later:

A *I felt as if I was walking with destiny, and that all my past life had been but a preparation for this hour and for this trial.*

Churchill was determined to lead the country to victory in the fight against Hitler:

B *. . . side by side, the British and French peoples have advanced to rescue not only Europe but mankind from the foullest and most soul-destroying tyranny which has ever darkened and stained the pages of history. Behind them — behind us — behind the Armies and Fleets of Britain and France — gather a group of shattered States and bludgeoned races: the Czechs, the Poles, the Norwegians, the Danes, the Dutch, the Belgians — upon all of whom the long night of barbarism will descend, unbroken even by a star of hope, unless we conquer, as conquer we must, as conquer we shall.*

C *This wicked man, the repository and embodiment of many forms of soul-destroying hatred, this monstrous product of former wrongs and shame, has now resolved to try to break our famous Island race by a process of indiscriminate slaughter and destruction. What he has done is to kindle a fire in British hearts, here and all over the world, which will glow long after all traces of the conflagration he has caused in London have been removed.*

From 1940 until the war ended in 1945, Churchill was an active and popular leader. Evidence **D** to **F** gives some clues as to why he was so successful.

Although the war lasted until 1945, for Churchill the real turning-point came in December 1941, when the Americans joined the Allies after the attack on Pearl Harbour. He wrote later:

G *. . . I knew the United States was in the war, up to the neck and in to the death. So we had won after all!. . . We had won the war, England would live; Britain would live; the Commonwealth of Nations and the Empire would live. How long the war would last or in what fashion it would end no man could tell, nor did I at this moment care. Once again in our long Island history we should emerge, however mauled or mutilated, safe and victorious. We should not be wiped out. Our history would not come to an end.*

After the war, Churchill suffered a surprise defeat in the 1945 general election. But he became Prime Minister again in 1951, and finally retired from politics in 1955.

??????????

1 Match each piece of evidence **A-F** with one of the following points about Churchill:
· broadcasting to the British people
· writing about the American entry into the war
· going on a morale-boosting tour of the troops
· feelings on becoming Prime Minister, May 1940
· commenting on the Blitz on London
· speaking on radio about the German conquest of Western Europe
· planning a campaign with his generals

2 What does each piece of evidence suggest about Churchill's strengths as a wartime leader?

3 If photographs **E** and **F** had been published in a German newspaper in 1942, what captions might the Nazi ministry of propaganda have given them? What signs suggest that they might be British propaganda photographs?

4 Imagine you were a reporter at any one of the scenes in **D**, **E** or **F**. What might Churchill have told you about what was happening, his hopes, feelings and plans?

IRELAND: THE EASTER RISING

1935. You go and stay with a friend near Dublin. On a wet afternoon you have:

A   . . . a chance to root then on the top of a wardrobe, in shoeboxes under a chest of drawers. I found a Sam Browne belt, thick with dust but complete with ammunition pouches, holster straps and all. The papers, photographs and clippings were rewarding. There were black bordered In Memoriam cards, too, with young men's faces and the names of battalions and brigades.

Later, you go for a bicycle ride. Along the roadside are crosses, with three letters – I.R.A.. carved on them. No one will talk about the graves or what they mean. Slowly you find out about the I.R.A. and the clues in **A**. They are about Ireland's history from 1900-22, when Southern Ireland, the Irish Republic, won its freedom from Britain. The struggle for independence was long, bitter and bloody. It split Ireland into two halves. Before 1922 *all* of Ireland was under British rule. A key event in the

B Timechart of the Easter Rising

1912	British Parliament passes an Act giving Ireland its own Parliament, which will run Irish affairs after 1914 (Home Rule). The Protestant leader Sir Edward Carson founds an armed force in Ulster, to fight for Protestant Ulster's right to go on being ruled from London.
1913	The Catholics set up an armed force – the Irish Volunteers – to fight for Home Rule.
1914	Start of the First World War. Irish troops go to fight for Britain.
1915-16	Leaders of the Irish Volunteers plan an uprising to fight for Irish Independence.
1916	**The Easter Rising** *24 April* 800 Irish Volunteers seize key government buildings in Dublin (the centre of British government in Ireland) they take over the General Post Office as their headquarters. The Irish Volunteers declare Ireland to be a Republic, free from British rule. *24-29 April* Bitter fighting in Dublin. About 2400 killed or wounded (from both sides). 180 buildings gutted or looted, **C**. The rising gains very little support from the people of Dublin – most of whom are Catholic. *29 April* Irish Volunteers surrender. 70 rebels sentenced to death. *3-12 May* British shoot rebel leaders.

Irish Republic's fight for independence was the Easter Rising of 1916. **B-G** are clues about the Easter Rising.

Although the rebel leaders were defeated, they defied their British captors. At his trial after the Rising, the Commander of the Irish Volunteer Force, P. H. Pearse, declared:

D *I stand over all my acts and words. When I was a child of ten I went down on my knees by my bedside one night and promised God that I should devote my life to an effort to free my country. I have kept that promise. . . If you strike us down now we shall rise again and renew the fight. You cannot conquer Ireland, you cannot extinguish the Irish passion for freedom. If our deed has not been sufficient to win freedom then our children will win it by a better deed.*

The British shot most of the Irish Volunteers' leaders. Father Aloysius was a Catholic priest. He was with James Connolly, a volunteer leader, when the British executed him. Father Aloysius tells us:

E *They carried him from his bed in an ambulance stretcher down to a waiting ambulance and drove him to Kilmainham Gaol. They carried him from the ambulance to the gaol yard and put him in a chair . . . and then they shot him.* (12 May 1916)

The Volunteer leaders became heroes, and the rebels who died in the fighting were glorified in songs like **F**.

F *My only son was shot in Dublin Fighting for his country bold. He fought for Ireland, Ireland only, The harp and shamrock, the green, white and gold.*

? ? ? ? ? ? ? ? ? ? ?

1 From the evidence on these pages, what events might the items in **A** be linked with? What does this suggest about the people who owned the house?

2 Look at **F**. What do the *harp*, *shamrock*, and *green, white and gold* represent? What message is the song trying to get across?

3 Use clues **B-F** to write a newspaper article either attacking or defending British action in Ireland in 1916. Begin: '*Easter 1916 saw. . .*'

4 How do you think the people of Eire (Southern Ireland) remember the Easter Rising? Why?

5 On 28 April 1916 a leader of the Irish Volunteers declared: '*Courage, boys, we are winning, and in the hour of victory let us not forget the splendid women who have stood by us. Never had man or woman a grander cause, never was a cause more grandly served.*'

Do you think he really believed they would win? Why might he have made this speech?

CIVIL WAR, 1918-23

After the First World War (1914-18) the key issue in Ireland was who should govern the country. There were three possible alternatives:

· Home Rule – Ireland to be self-governing but within the British Commonwealth
· A fully independent Irish Republic – a self-governing state with no king or queen
· A divided Ireland – the South to be independent, the North to remain part of Great Britain.

B **Major events in the Civil War, 1919-23**

1919	*January* Sinn Fein declares independence from Britain. I.R.A. attack British police barracks and army depots, killing armed policemen and soldiers.
1920	*March* The Black and Tans (mostly soldiers who had fought in the First World War) arrive from Britain to fight the I.R.A.
1920	British Parliament passes the Government of Ireland Act: Ulster to have its own Home Rule parliament in Belfast and Sinn Fein to have the same in Dublin. Sinn Fein rejects this.
1920-21	Vicious civil war between Black and Tans and I.R.A. 60 000 British troops in Ireland.
1921	*May* Sinn Fein wins sweeping victory in the Irish General Election. *July* British and Sinn Fein sign truce. *December* Sinn Fein and British sign treaty setting up Irish Free State in Southern Ireland. This is to be a member of the Commonwealth, and all Irish MPs must sign an oath of loyalty to the British Crown. Ulster to stay within the United Kingdom.
1922	*January* The Irish Free State Parliament accepts the treaty by 64 votes to 57.
1922-23	*June-May* Civil War in Southern Ireland between Free Staters and Republicans. Free Staters execute 77 I.R.A. leaders. Free Staters win war.

In December 1918 there was a general election. Of the new MPs, 73 belonged to Sinn Fein (the Republican party), 26 were Unionists (in favour of the North remaining part of Britain) and 6 supported Home Rule.

In January 1919 the 73 Sinn Fein MPs decided to set up their own parliament in Dublin. They wanted to create an Irish Republic like the one declared during the Easter Rising (see page 60). They claimed:

A   . . . *the power to make laws binding on the people of Ireland, and that the Irish Parliament is the only Parliament to which that people will give its allegiance.*

The British Government refused to accept Sinn Fein's claims. War broke out, and two years of fighting followed, **B**. The Irish Republican Army (I.R.A.) fought against the Royal Irish Constabulary (R.I.C.) and a band of British ex-soldiers, who were nick-named the 'Black and Tans' because of their khaki army tops and black trousers (the Black and Tans were a famous pack of foxhounds).

The fighting was bitter and bloody. **C** shows the village of Balbriggan after the Black and Tans

C

had raided it. I.R.A. men set the railway carriages in **D** on fire. **E**, written 40 years after the war, describes the sorts of things that happened:

E   *Thomas MacCurtain was Lord Mayor of Cork and an I.R.A. officer. Men with blackened faces burst into his house at night and killed him at his bedroom door. The coroner's jury returned a verdict of wilful murder against three inspectors of the R.I.C. . . One of the inspectors was called Swanzy. They got him away to Lisburn in Antrim. Some months later an actor friend of mine was standing on a street in (Lisburn) talking to Joe McKelvey, an I.R.A. commandant from Belfast. Soon the inspector appeared on the far side of the street. McKelvey shouted, 'Hey, you, Swanzy' 'Me? What?' he said, turning. 'This is for MacCurtain,' said McKelvey, and hit him with most of a Mauser pistol clip. My actor friend's part was to cover McKelvey and slip him out of town. His own pistol was dripping wet from sweat. Outside Lisburn, the actor gave the guns to two girls who hid them in their bloomers. . .*

In January 1922 the Sinn Fein MPs agreed to make a treaty with the British. Ulster (the North) was to remain part of Great Britain. The South was to become an independent state — the Irish Free State — within the British Commonwealth.

As part of the treaty, all Irish MPs had to swear an oath of loyalty to the British King and Commonwealth. Many of the Sinn Fein MPs refused to swear. This caused a split between them and the I.R.A. A bitter civil war followed in the south, between the Free Staters and the Republicans, with terrible acts on both sides:

F   *There were many republican prisoners in Tralee jail, Kerry. In the morning the Free State soldiers took out nine of them and put them in a lorry. One had a broken wrist from the beatings and another a broken arm. Beside Ballyseedy Wood there was a tree lying across the road. The nine men were taken out of the lorry and tied with an electric flex in a circle around the tree. . There was a mine next to the tree and the soldiers exploded it.*

Fathers and sons, friends and neighbours had become enemies and were fighting each other. In the end, the Free Staters won — but all the Irish people had suffered.

Since 1922 Ireland has been divided between the South and the North. In the North, Ulster, Protestants rule. Ulster is part of Britain. In 1969 began a period of violence in Ulster, which has lasted until today. Catholics in Ulster demanded political rights and a fair share of jobs in the province. Some Catholics, the I.R.A., wanted Union with the South. The result has been a civil war in which thousands have died, for Protestants refused to give Catholics in the North a say in the government of Ulster.

? ? ? ? ? ? ? ? ? ? ?

1 Who or what were:
  a Sinn Fein
  b the I.R.A.
  c the R.I.C.
  d the Black and Tans
  e the Irish Free State?

2 Make up newspaper headings for photographs **C** and **D**, from both a pro-Sinn Fein and a pro-British point of view.

3 Imagine you are one of the people in **C**. Write about what happened when the Black and Tans raided your village.

4 You interview Swanzy's ghost, **E**; What does he tell you about the Civil War, his part in MacCurtain's death, his own death?

QUIZ TIME